Praise for

Treating People Not Patients

"Michael Sonick's *business* is to use his medical expertise to keep dental patients healthy. But he's acutely aware that his deeper *calling* is to use his hospitality gifts to make people feel better. That insight no doubt separates his practice from the pack, and his lessons are applicable to any customer-facing business."

—Danny Meyer
Restaurateur, Gramercy Tavern,
Union Square Café, Shake Shack

"Dr. Mike Sonick's book *Treating People Not Patients* is a call to action for the future of medicine. It is rare to find a master surgeon who understands the importance of human connection in healing. Mike shares an enjoyable blend of true stories and specific teachings that model what being an extraordinary healthcare provider really means."

—Peter H. Diamandis, MD
Founder of XPRIZE, A360,
Singularity University, and Author of *Abundance,*
Bold, Future Is Faster than You Think, and *Life Force*

"Dr. Sonick's book is a reminder, particularly for those in medicine and dentistry, that individuals are at the core of any business model—something many practitioners seem to have forgotten. Using powerful stories from his life and practice, he shows the necessity of improving the quality of the patient-doctor human connection and makes a case for a customer-centered and hospitality-driven approach to treating patients."

—Dan Sullivan
Founder, Strategic Coach®, and *Wall Street Journal* and *USA Today* Bestselling Author

"In the age of constantly advancing technology, human interaction has unfortunately become more and more impersonal. This book, written by Dr. Michael Sonick, represents a timely affirmation of the importance of the human connection. I love the way he utilized insights of his interactions to help the reader carve their own path to unforgettable personal connections. I hope that this book will provide you with the ability to link your own clinical excellence and consider ways to incorporate that excellence into providing memorable and long-lasting relationships. This book has become a must-read at the Kois Center."

—John C. Kois, DMD, MSD
Founder and Director of The Kois Center, University of Washington School of Dentistry, Affiliate Professor at the Graduate Restorative Program, and Consulting Editor for *The Compendium of Continuing Education in Dentistry*

"Dr. Mike Sonick's *Treating People Not Patients* is a welcomed, comprehensive treatise on how to create an environment of trust, respect, and healing that is an invaluable read for any physician. Culture trumps strategy, but it's really nice having both in your arsenal! Mike appreciates that providing the best possible care combines the proper ethos and professionalism with personalized, humanistic care in a welcoming environment. Surgical outcomes will always shine when provided in such a manner."

—**Stuart Zarich, MD**
Chief of Cardiology, Bridgeport Hospital; Director of Joel
E Smilow Heart Institute; and Associate Clinical Professor
of Medicine at Yale University School of Medicine

"Dr. Michael Sonick's book *Treating People Not Patients* takes customer experience to new heights. Through his own experience and examples, you'll discover a deep understanding of serving people, not just solving their problems. This book is an invaluable resource on practice management for anyone in dentistry, medicine, or business at large. By picking up a copy of this book, you'll be on track to offering the best possible experience for your patients and the people on your team."

—**Dr. Kary Oberbrunner**
Wall Street Journal and *USA Today* Bestselling Author
and CEO of Igniting Souls Publishing Agency

"Dr. Sonick has captured the bellwether of success in administering clinical practice. Through his vast experience, his learnings are shared through anecdotes, personal reflection, and strategic communication skills necessary to engage the binding trust that creates subjective value for our patients."

—**Robert A. Faiella, DMD, MMSc, MBA**
Past President, American Dental Association

"It is very gratifying to both physician and patient to establish long-term relationships. Trust grows from such relationships and allows for detection of changes in health, both physical and mental. *Treating People Not Patients* provides insights into this important concept."

—Jean Bolognia, MD
Professor of Dermatology, Yale University School of Medicine

"Dr. Michael Sonick, a master clinician, realizes that clinical skills alone do not guarantee success. Dr. Sonick is a master at understanding human behavior and shares the challenges and solutions to creating a successful team, which we at Ferrazzi Greenlight call Co-Elevation. *Treating People Not Patients* holds the blueprint to creating more meaning, freedom, and prosperity in your profession."

—Keith Ferrazzi
#1 *New York Times* Bestselling Author;
Chairman, Ferrazzi Greenlight

"This wonderful book by Michael shows how dedicated he is as a human being to treating his patients with grace and humility. Besides having great surgical capabilities, Michael has always been a warm and passionate human being. It should always remind us that we are not just doing procedures, but we are treating people. Too many times we forget that, and Michael's book is a perfect reminder that we should always remember that people come first; procedures just help them."

—Dr. Dennis Tarnow
Clinical Professor of Periodontology and Director of
Implant Education, Columbia School of Dental Medicine

"I've tried to articulate Dr. Sonick's philosophy to a number of people . . . but never in a fully thought-out way. We must not forget that healing involves more than a surgical procedure or taking a pill; it involves a human relationship. This book is a timely reminder to pause and realize that there is a person on the other side of our procedures. Bravo, Dr. Sonick, for taking the time to write this."

—Scott W. Wolfe, MD
Chief Emeritus Upper Extremity Surgery, Hospital for
Special Surgery, New York, New York

"Dr. Sonick is that rare individual who serves heart first, title second. He sees the patient before him as a *human*... someone who presents more than a clinical need; someone who needs to be addressed as a whole person. With a deep understanding that care is both a noun and a verb, Dr. Sonick puts his patients at ease by delivering the quality they expect while effectively communicating the personal purpose that drives his work. His humble and genuine approach allows patients to both know *and* feel they are in the capable, caring hands of a fellow *human*. This book is an indispensable guide to creating human experiences that foster loyalty, alleviate worry, and lift you far above the competition."

—Todd Williams
Healthcare and Hospitality Advisor; Former Senior
Learning Manager, Four Seasons Hotels and Resorts;
Former Vice President, Culture Development,
Centura Health

"In *Treating People Not Patients,* Dr. Mike Sonick clearly articulates a people-centric approach to healing, utilizing a series of proven strategies and procedures. It is rare to hear a master surgeon detail so meticulously his philosophy of providing human-centered patient care. If you practice medicine or dentistry, or are involved in any aspect of customer service, this book is an essential read."

—Gino Wickman
Bestselling Author of *Traction* and *The EOS Life*

"Dr. Sonick's book is a reminder that people are at the core of any business model, and particularly those in medicine and dentistry—something many practitioners seem to have forgotten. With powerful stories from his life and practice, he makes a case for a humanistic and hospitality-driven approach to caring for others, something so many of us sorely need."

—Mike Koenigs
Serial Entrepreneur, Speaker, Influencer, and 13-time #1
Bestselling Author

"*Treating People Not Patients* fills a significant void in dental education, providing a detailed and brilliant treatise on practice management and patient relations. Dentists are trained in the necessary skills to provide treatment to their patients, but this new book by a well-known, successful periodontist brings his experience and skills in patient management to the fore with a sensibility that has not been equaled to date.

This book is a must-read for full-time practitioners young and old."

—**Thomas E. Van Dyke, DDS, PhD**
Vice President and Senior Member of Staff, Forsyth Institute; Professor of Oral Medicine, Infection and Immunity, Faculty of Medicine, Harvard University

"*Treating People Not Patients* is an exceptional work from the humble master Dr. Mike Sonick. Mike shares his deep-rooted philosophy of serving humans consistently with empathy and care, all the while managing the complex nuances of running a successful dental practice. This captivating book will revolutionize the way medical care is delivered and hopefully bring about a paradigm shift in the management and development of human capital. The goal is to focus on our most important commodity—people."

—**Dr. Ratnadeep Patil, Bds, PhD**
Smile Care India, Mumbai, India

"Mastering relationships is the shortcut to success, and Mike is definitely an expert on this topic. Modern consumers want more than just a good dental treatment; people today expect unique experiences, so we shouldn't miss the opportunities to learn more about how to create meaningful moments in our daily work. In this art, Mike is a master."

—**Christian Coachman**
Founder and CEO of Digital Smile Design

"I was told in medical school that 'bedside manner' could not be taught. This book, written by a master clinician educator, completely dispelled that myth for me. Even the most experienced practitioner cannot truly be a healer without a personal connection to his or her patient. Michael teaches us that this connection begins even before the medical encounter and extends until well after it is over. A must for anyone who cares for patients in any capacity."

—Mark Lachs, MD
Professor of Medicine, Weill Cornell Medicine
and Director of Geriatric Medicine, New York Presbyterian
Health Care

"Dr. Mike Sonick is a master clinician and an outstanding teacher. In *Treating People Not Patients*, he introduces the often-overlooked concepts of human connection, which are at the heart of every doctor–patient interaction. *Treating People Not Patients* is a how-to guide to take it to the next level in clinical practice."

—Dr. Maurice Salama
Founder, Dental XP, Atlanta, Georgia

"Dr. Michael Sonick's book *Treating People Not Patients* is a much-needed treatise. As someone who has been in the hospitality industry, as well as written a TedX talk on the effects of hospitality, I often speak about how the needs in the medical and dental industry, as well as other industries, should also wear the yolk of hospitality upon their shoulders as much as any fine dining establishment. Michael speaks to the core of this and how important it is. Putting an implant into an 18-year-old that has to last 60 years is wildly more important than a Friday night reservation. I can only hope that Michael's book will inspire other health care providers to see it as a people-first, not a patient-first, industry. We would all be the beneficiaries."

—Bobby Stuckey
Partner and Master Sommelier, Frasca Hospitality Group
and James Beard Award for Outstanding Service

"I'm a patient of Michael's and, in my spare time, CEO of a $500 million a year chain of family food and liquor stores. Treating people is the key to any business, whether medical, dental, hospitality, or even grocery. This book nails it!"

—Stew Leonard
CEO, Stew Leonard's

"Dr. Michael Sonick is a compassionate leader when treating his patients and guiding his staff. Mike has what I call VLP (Vision, Love, and Patience). Mike has the Vision to guide his practice to what he wishes to accomplish. He has Love for his patients, employees, and his life's work. He exhibits the Patience to understand the journey he is on with his patients and his team, as well as the ability to make the necessary adjustments to stay true to his goal. Dr. Sonick's compassion and clarity as a leader, doctor, and mentor are evidently expressed in his newest book. If you wish to emulate one of the best, I urge you to read this book."

—Bill Raveis
Real Estate Entrepreneur

TREATING PEOPLE
NOT PATIENTS

TREATING PEOPLE NOT PATIENTS

Transformational Insights on Hospitality and Human Connection to Provide High-Quality Care Experiences for People and Practitioners

Michael Sonick, DMD

ethos
collective

Printed in the United States of America

Published by Ethos Collective™
PO Box 43, Powell, OH 43065
www.EthosCollective.vip

LCCN: 2022916562
Paperback ISBN: 978-1-63680-095-0
Hardcover ISBN: 978-1-63680-096-7
E-book ISBN: 978-1-63680-097-4

Available in paperback, hardcover, e-book, and audiobook

Any internet addresses (websites, blogs, etc.) and telephone numbers printed in this book are offered as a resource. They are not intended in any way to be or imply an endorsement by Ethos Collective, nor does Ethos Collective vouch for the content of these sites and numbers for the life of this book.

Some names and identifying details have been changed to protect the privacy of individuals.

To my wife, Carole, for her unselfish love and
undying encouragement.

You have made our journey so much more fun.
To my beautiful children, Becky, Jason, and Jenn, you make
me prouder than you could even know. I love you all.

Contents

Foreword

The heartbeat of virtually every successful business is consumer loyalty. But consumers seeking goods and services across industries—including health care—often find themselves faced with a plethora of choices. If and when they choose to engage your business, they will have formed an expectation about the service they will receive. How?

Before they choose your business, they have already had numerous touchpoints from you, during which they have considered how the experience is likely to go.

In such a competitive market, building loyalty demands frictionless interactions from the moment your consumer encounters your operation. That means it is up to you to make your consumers feel they matter and that their business is important to you. In addition to keeping them, you will create advocates, or "raving fans," people who not only forgive mistakes more readily and are far less price sensitive but who also refer you to others. That is as true in medicine and dentistry as it is in any other field, but it is something many physicians and dentists have forgotten—or never learned at all.

Dr. Mike Sonick takes that insight to heart. Inspired by leaders in the hospitality industry, from Danny Meyer to Nina and Tim Zagat and the Four Seasons, he has built a practice that prioritizes the patient experience—and has been since he first opened his doors.

But brand loyalty is not just about the people purchasing your service; it is also about the people delivering your service. In most cases, the people who provide those first touchpoints—from a consumer's very first interaction with your business—are generally among the lowest paid and the least trained, and yet the impression they leave on the consumer has a tremendous impact on whether they will choose you.

Because the people delivering your service *are* your brand, your work to cultivate consumer loyalty must start with them. You must establish a culture of continuous improvement and set key performance indicators (KPIs) at every stage of the consumer relationship to reduce turnover and raise your reputation. Ultimately, you must understand that both the members of your team and those you treat are people. That is the thesis of Dr. Sonick's book.

Intentionally developing your people to be your ambassadors will build loyalty not only among your consumers but also among the very individuals charged with delivering your service. And that means you have to get into the details, just as the general manager of a fine restaurant or elegant hotel would do. You need to know how long the average wait time is to book an appointment, how many times the phone rings before it is answered, how long the consumer is typically put on hold, and how long patients wait to be cared for once they enter your building. These metrics are foundational in building a hospitality culture in your business.

Surveys provide another avenue for assessment and improvement, measuring the people experience. But with notoriously low response rates, you must outperform consumer expectations to motivate them to share feedback. Further, as Dr. Sonick explains, you must do something with the feedback you amass.

In a service culture, most feedback will be praise for your people. As with any other business improvement process, that feedback must be benchmarked and then converted into action, particularly through employee reward and recognition programs. Reviewing your consumer feedback with your teams—regardless of role—highlights the fact that every person in the consumer interaction is vital to the overall success of the business. Recognizing those who deliver excellent service underscores the importance of people to your culture and is key to retaining talent.

Additionally, as a leader, you must set the standard, both with your consumers as well as your team. Your personal touch is invaluable in building relationships and loyalty. Dr. Sonick sets a wonderful example, making a habit of recognizing patients and staff alike. He personally checks in on every patient after procedures and sends handwritten thank-you notes to the team members who receive positive feedback. It's evidence that he is committed to a culture of caring and inspires his team to turn around and do the same for those they serve.

Dr. Sonick knows establishing a culture of continual refinement through the intentional and caring development of your people is critical for remaining a best-in-class organization—with raving fans—and *Treating People Not Patients* serves as a guide on how to do just that.

—Scott Davis
President and CEO of FLIK Hospitality Group
Division of Compass Group

Acknowledgments

I have been in love with the concept of treating people, not patients, throughout my entire career.

The approach was instilled in me at a very young age. And like most people, my primary influences were my parents, Joanne and Jay Sonick. They valued hard work and being kind, courageous, and true to your words and beliefs, and they taught me to do the same. Thanks to them, being of service to others has always been a calling.

I have been fortunate to have been mentored professionally by teachers whom I did not consciously choose. Dr. Harald Löe, dean of the University of Connecticut School of Medicine and the father of modern periodontology, made an indelible impression on me the first day of dental school. He addressed us as physicians of the oral cavity and instilled in us the belief that we were to treat the whole patient, not just their mouths. This was (and still is) a revolutionary concept in dentistry. We were required to be comprehensive in our care and see people, not procedures. I did not know it at the time, but Dr. Löe—the most impactful periodontist in the world—would forever shape the way I approached patient care.

I was also fortunate to study in concert with both medical and dental students. Forty years later, I maintain close relationships with many of my classmates. These close colleagues, whom I can call on at any time for advice or consult, include Drs. David Rosania, Jim Bergman, Robert Noonan, Bill Cappiello, Barry Messinger, Jeffrey Thompson, Richard Lasnier, Jay Krompinger, Jim Dobbin, Jack Ryan, Eileen Reale, John Papale, Craig Leffingwell, and Chris Dickens.

I am grateful to Dr. Myron Finkel, whom I had the privilege of working for at age twenty-seven. He gave me my first private practice gig in a Manhattan townhouse on the Upper East Side. His words, "It's Showtime," echo in my head every morning as I enter my clinic. They help me remember that it's not about me. Instead, I'm there to support the people who trust me with their well-being and their livelihoods.

My true passion for clinical patient care was not evident until I attended Emory University in Atlanta for my residency. Fortuitously, two soon-to-be international scientific icons would become my mentors: Drs. Tom Van Dyke and Steven Offenbacher. They showed me the value of having a scientific basis for all of my clinical work.

Doctor Abe Shuster took me under his wing and schooled me in the refined and delicate work of performing cosmetic surgical procedures at a time when few were aesthetically focused. I was also fortunate to have been taught clinically by Drs. Ralph Gray, Colin Richman, and Michael Fritz. Thank you, Dr. Gerald Kramer, who was taken from us far too early. You set the bar for clinical excellence. Thank you, Dr. Myron Nevins, for carrying that message forward. You are generous beyond words.

I will always be indebted to Dr. Dennis Tarnow, whom I met at NYU during my first year in periodontal private practice in 1984. He taught me to be a more thoughtful dentist and more impactful teacher.

At NYU, Paul Fletcher, Dr. Tarnow's partner, introduced me to Ken Beacham, Assistant Dean and Director of Clinical Education, who gave me the opportunity to travel and to teach dentists around the world. Together, we have visited and taught on six continents—a real gift.

Thank you, Ken Varner, for believing in me and giving me the opportunity to develop out-of-the-box educational programs that engage and empower.

Teaching at NYU and having close professional relationships with Manhattan dentists for the past four decades has placed me in contact with some of the masters in our field, including Dr. Jeff Shapiro; my longtime friend and colleague Frank Celenza; Vinnie Celenza; Burt Langer; Ziad Jalbout; Jason Kim; Mazen Natour; Dean Vafiadis; Johnathan Levine; and countless others. Thank you all.

I have been fortunate to have been mentored by some of the greatest clinicians and teachers in the world. Thank you, Dr. Michael Pikos, P. D. Miller, Craig Misch, John Kois, Gerald Chiche, Robert Marges, David Garber, Maurice Salama, Markus Hurzeler, Otto Zuhr, Istvan Urban, Eduardo Anitua, Michael Block, George Priest, Jay Smith, Steven Locascio, Pascal Magne, Brian Mealey, George Mandelaris, William Robbins, Greg Toback and Christian Coachman. Your wisdom has enlightened me beyond measure.

I want to acknowledge the original and current members of my mastermind group, the Secret Study Club, for openly sharing everything about your businesses and your lives. The impact of our group is immeasurable. Thank you, Drs. Robert Levine, Bobby Butler, Jeffrey Thomas, Bradley McAllister, Jeff Ganales, Robert Faiella, Rui Ma, Stephanie Koo, Phil Fava, Fred Norkin, Lilly Aranguren, Thomas

Eshraghi, Justin Zalewsky, Alan Farber, Monish Bhola, Mitch Godat, Grant King, Jennifer Doobrow, David Rosania, and Sam Bakuri.

My clinical mentors have made a tremendous impact upon my career. However, the impetus for writing this book came from Danny Meyer, author of *Setting the Table* and one of the most successful restaurateurs in Manhattan. His concept of enlightened hospitality has had more of an influence on the way in which we run our dental clinic than any other mentor. From him I learned that everything comes back to creating meaningful relationships. Thank you, Danny.

I must thank Dan Sullivan, my coach, who introduced me to the concept of Unique Ability®, which has led me to live a life of freedom.

Thank you, Julie Waller and Kristi Chambers for nudging me along when I get stuck in the gap.

To Michael Hall, who unwittingly changed my life when he read my Culture Index™ to a crowd of 400 people, you have my sincere gratitude. It was the key that helped unlock the door to living my best life.

I will always be indebted to Peter Diamandis for introducing me to a world of technological abundance and for keeping me apprised of the possibility of living a longer, healthier, happier, more meaningful life.

I want to acknowledge Stuart Zarich, my workout partner of twenty-two years. Thank you for showing up two or three days a week, every week. Thank you for listening to me ramble on about dentistry, medicine, people, changing the world, accepting the world, making a difference… you have been an unbelievable friend.

I would like to thank Jose Campos, my creative director. You are an artistic genius and an invaluable colleague. You make everything you touch look better. Thank you, Ariel

Hubbard, for your editorial assistance and for being a sounding board throughout COVID as this project took shape. I respect your input and the voice you gave my work.

And finally, I would never have accomplished any of this without the support of my wife, Carole. Thank you for reading all of this, listening to me, offering suggestions, and loving this work into existence. I do not say it enough, but I do appreciate you, for everything.

Introduction

Lifeguard. Cocktail pianist. Furniture deliveryman. Bartender. I've been a periodontist for over four decades, but before that, I held a host of other jobs. And to date, one of the most impactful was my stint as a waiter.

Waiting tables taught me that it takes more than one skill to thrive in the restaurant industry. I quickly learned that it wasn't just about accurately capturing an order or delivering plates to a table in a timely fashion; it was also about delivering an excellent experience.

Anyone who has been to a restaurant understands that even more important than the quality of the food is the social interaction that occurs during the meal—both between diners and between diners and the waitstaff. Just take a moment to consider the truly memorable meals you've had and how many times the service you received played a role. The experience itself becomes more than the sum of its parts, and you're left with a feeling that lasts long past dessert.

Those who have experienced a great meal don't just talk about a perfect filet or the thrill of Space Mountain; they talk about how it made them feel. About how invigorated they were to be eating *jamón ibérico* and sipping *sangría* with the most charming waitstaff in Barcelona, Spain, or the sense of calm that washed over them as they shared the freshest seafood they'd ever experienced with their spouse, overlooking the ocean on the coast of California. The value of those experiences isn't limited to hospitality. It extends to a multitude of environments, including medicine and dentistry.

Over the course of my career, I've realized that clinical excellence is only one factor in building a successful medical or dental practice. The other is indeed hospitality—helping patients feel comfortable and at home alongside the excellent care I was trained to deliver.

It is my job not only to be competent, but also to make sure patients feel cared for and nurtured and know that they came to the right place. I have to make sure they understand that, from the moment they walk through my doors, they will be taken care of, that they know they are safe.

It's one of the most important lessons I have learned to date, and it's why I've written this book. But in these pages, you won't find a typical guide to customer service—or even how to run a successful practice. Instead, you'll find a collection of stories and insights that highlight what an excellent experience entails, and some of the details to consider when creating one in your operation.

After being in practice for so long, I have become very competent at carrying out procedures. I am fortunate enough to enjoy my work and the science behind it—alongside the art and craftsmanship it entails. I appreciate the challenge of performing a complex bone reconstruction procedure or an implant surgery. I find the tasks of treating infection to be quite gratifying, especially since oral health has an impact on physical health at large. But more than anything, I know that I'm not just in the dental business; I'm in the business of improving the quality of patients' lives. In fact, that's our practice's mission—to improve the quality of patients' lives-something you'll read a lot more about in these pages.

Our mission says nothing about dentistry or medicine. What it does speak to is the people we serve and what we help do for them on a grand scale.

When I treat an eighteen-year-old, placing a dental implant, for instance, I know their life expectancy may be nearing ninety years of age. My work has to last at least sixty years, and thus, I'm staring into their future, hoping to make it a better one with less pain. The same goes for those in their thirties or forties. The work I do now, from both a clinical and an educational perspective, will help ensure that they don't have to worry about bone loss, significant infections, and even some systemic diseases.

Although the procedures and lessons that support that brighter future are relatively simple—how to brush and floss one's teeth, the importance of regular cleanings, and more—the impact of my work has the potential to be much greater: A life free of suffering and pain and bolstered by confidence. That starts with a sense of empathy.

Caring for my patients—and caring about their experience—begins with a willingness to walk in their shoes and recognize that the best-quality care is not about fearmongering or wearing a white coat to signal one's authority but about hospitality.

One of my patients, Ashok Ahuja, a successful businessperson, told me that to do well in business you must have integrity, humility, capability, charisma, and—of course—empathy. To me, those are key ingredients in hospitality too.

And when you put them to work, an effort that is as much about passion and process as it is about building the right habits, everything changes. You establish trust. You create loyalty. And most importantly, you enable those you serve to feel in control of their path and their progress. That is a powerful gift.

In addition, you'll find, as I did, that the kinds of experiences I described aren't limited to those in the hospitality industry or even the medical field but to any and every type of business and to virtually every role there is.

With that in mind, I hope this book serves you, your team, and the meaningful people in your life by providing an ethos by which to practice—and to live.

Salud!

1

Showtime

Improving the Patient Experience through Hospitality

O n arrival, my guests typically notice the immaculate landscaping: a perfectly manicured lawn, knockout rosebushes that burst with blooms seven months of the year. When they walk through the door, a warm and caring staff member immediately greets them. Our guests often comment on the space—the fresh paint on the walls, new carpeting, pristine ceiling tiles, modern décor—which gets updated every three years or so. As they scan the framed articles on display, they learn about our accomplishments and innovations. Soft, relaxing music lends calmness to the space. Before they are whisked off to their seat, someone offers them a selection of coffee, tea, and soft drinks.

As I write this, we are in the middle of the COVID-19 pandemic. Elements of that experience have of course

1

changed, but we aim to capture that same sense of calm and care we have always provided, making guests feel that, at least within our four walls, all is normal. Today, the seamless greeting includes screening for symptoms using a digital form, a quick temperature check, and the offer of hand sanitizer before they are seated.

No one ever waits long for service, and we welcome them to stay as long as they like. Many have been returning for years. They rave about the experience, sending their family members, friends, and colleagues in to try it for themselves.

What kind of service, exactly, am I providing? This experience is what I offer everyone who walks through the doors of Fairfield County Implants and Periodontics, a full-service dental care center in Fairfield, Connecticut. If it sounds more like a fine dining experience, that's intentional. We've modeled our customer experience after the kind created by famed restaurateur Danny Meyer.

Danny Meyer opened his first restaurant, Union Square Café, in 1985—the same year I opened my first practice. I've followed his career since the beginning as he added Gramercy Tavern, The Modern, Maialino, and nearly twenty other restaurants to his portfolio—along with hundreds of Shake Shacks. All the while, he has prioritized his employees, pioneering an initiative called Hospitality Included, which folds the gratuity into menu prices to better compensate restaurant teams.

The guest experience has always been of the utmost importance to Meyer. His unique approach has resulted in twenty-eight James Beard Awards for his company and numerous accolades recognizing his capability and commitment as a restaurateur and civic leader. As he wrote in *Setting the Table*, his best-selling memoir and business book,

Hospitality is the foundation of my business philosophy. Virtually nothing else is as important as how one is made to feel in any business transaction. Hospitality exists when you believe the other person is on your side. The converse is just as true. Hospitality is present when something happens for you. It is absent when something happens to you. Those two simple prepositions—for and to—*express it all.*[1]

Danny Meyer became a mentor of sorts. His impressive career and unique insights helped to guide me toward my vision with a totally different, yet highly applicable, frame of reference. I'm not bringing home James Beard Awards or modernizing the roadside burger stand like he did, but I have long been dedicated to providing those I serve with what Danny refers to as *enlightened hospitality*—a soulful and caring approach to service. In our practice, hospitality is evident in every patient interaction, from the way we look, to the words we use, the tone of our voice, and the integrity and respect with which we operate. It is evident in the way we make our patients feel.

A Hospitable Start

I owe just as much, if not more, of my philosophy on hospitality in practice to another mentor I met early in my career. One year out of dental school and fresh out of a hospital-based surgical residency at Metropolitan Hospital in Spanish Harlem, I began working in a series of clinics in Manhattan. Each encouraged me to practice dentistry in a way that didn't sit right with me. The higher-ups urged me to speed through patients, racking up procedures along the way. Why? So the owners could make more money.

3

Those owners weren't doctors; they were businesspeople—and that was evident. Shortly after my first day at the last clinic in which I'd work, I watched the owner step from his Rolls-Royce, adjusting the sleeves of his fancy suit as he made his way across the parking lot. "Keep up the good work," he said, patting me on the shoulder as he brushed by.

But I couldn't. I refused to perform bad dentistry. My father, Jay Sonick, had taught me to value hard work and raised me with a tremendous sense of integrity. He told me over and over again that my word is my bond, that I should never lie. Day after day in that clinic, those lessons echoed in my head. Despite the pressure to rush people along, I worked carefully and methodically. When my overseers told me to pick up the pace to increase production, I didn't. Eventually, the office manager fired me.

I wasn't upset. I hadn't liked working at that clinic, or in any of the clinics I had been in before it. By then, I was two years out of dental school with a yearlong residency at Metropolitan Hospital under my belt. I had not yet become a periodontist. I didn't have much experience, but I was sure an ideal job was out there. I just had to find it.

Then, one fateful day, I saw an ad in the local dental journal. An Upper East Side practice was looking for a dentist.

Now, back in 1981, the Upper East Side of Manhattan was a very exclusive neighborhood with a certain elegance. Unlike the clinic that had just fired me, an actual dentist owned the practice, Dr. Myron Finkel. He needed help because he had broken his back in a cab accident on the way to the opera. The accident was about as dramatic as he was.

My interview took place in one of the patient rooms at Mt. Sinai Hospital in Manhattan. When I walked into his room, Myron was reclined in the bed surrounded by balloons. Visitors, close friends just chatting away, occupied both chairs. The fact that he wore a full back brace didn't keep things from feeling like a party. Myron's zest for life drew joyful people to him.

At that time, I was a twenty-seven-year-old kid without a clear path. I had just come back from Israel where I had spent the summer volunteering on *kibbutzim*. I didn't know I would develop the passion I now have for the dental profession. I didn't know I wanted to become a periodontist. I did know I wanted a life full of meaning and contribution, all while having fun. So did Myron.

We connected immediately because we shared a similar outlook. It turned out that he was also passionate about Israel. After about thirty minutes of conversation, he said, "You know, I really like you. You have the job." His friend Mike, who was occupying one of the chairs and also happened to be a dentist, gave him a look of disbelief. He clearly did not share Myron's commitment to this unknown young dentist after such a brief meeting.

"Okay," I said, hoping he wasn't just looking for a temporary replacement because of the vulnerability he must have felt with a broken back in a hospital.

"I'll pay you 40 percent of what you collect. You start on Monday." With that, he threw me the keys to his office. There were no papers to sign. He didn't even know my phone number. Hesitancy radiated off me. Myron picked up on it and softened his offer slightly. "Just take a look at the office," he said. "If you like it, you'll start."

His office occupied the first floor of a townhouse at 161 East 64th Street, between Lexington and Third. Our neighbors were Arthur Schlesinger and Mary Tyler Moore. Richard and Pat Nixon lived right across the street, adjacent to the office's garden where we could spend our lunch hour.

When I walked in the door that first Monday, I learned that Myron had an assistant, a receptionist, a dental hygienist, and now me. I had minimal work experience outside my residency, and now I was managing his Upper East Side practice with no guidance whatsoever. As soon as Myron got out of the hospital, he went directly to Israel to recuperate. For three months, I was on my own.

When he returned to the office, he still couldn't work. So, he began mentoring me. With plenty of time on his hands and very little mobility, he reviewed everything I did. He didn't know it at the time, but with attention and guidance, he made more of an impact on me than anyone in my dental career.

He was a larger-than-life New York character, inhabiting a world like the one Damon Runyon wrote about. Our clientele included models, Broadway stars, members of the gay community, and mobsters he'd grown up with in Red Hook, Brooklyn. Myron was smart—he had graduated at the top of his class at NYU. He was dramatic; he loved the theater and anyone and everyone in the business. And he had the ability to connect with anyone.

It was the early 1980s—a time when practically anything went. He practiced in jeans and a white jacket. Sometimes he would walk into the treatment room with a corncob pipe in his mouth. But unlike my childhood dentist, who frequently smoked through my appointments, he always put it down before going to work. He was a good dentist and a good businessman. Patients loved him.

Myron was in love with the stage. Though he wasn't an actor, he was a performer in his own right. Every day, Myron would come into the office, turn to me, and say, **"Mike, it's showtime."** In the office, we were like actors on stage. Our dental school training, continuing education, and any mentoring we received counted as rehearsal. Any day-to-day preparation happened behind the scenes, or backstage—making notes, taking a sip of water, even checking in with our loved ones. He reminded me often that patients weren't concerned about how we were feeling, whether we had a headache or were navigating a divorce. Like an audience, they came to us for a single purpose. Although entertainment wasn't the sole reason for their visit, it helped to eliminate their worries for the time they were in our care. Just as an audience member would, they were paying a premium for our services, and it was our job to make them feel that they mattered.

It's Showtime

If you are a dentist or physician, it is essential to keep in mind that, although you may have done a particular procedure hundreds or even thousands of times (I've placed ten thousand implants over the course of my career), this may be your patients' first and only time experiencing it. It's your responsibility to ensure your guests enjoy a perfectly pristine, well-orchestrated, stress-free experience. For them, you must put on a show. You are the Nathan Lane or Bernadette Peters of the examination room.

When I walk into the treatment room to begin a procedure, patients typically ask me how I'm doing. What they really want to know is whether I'm ready to perform. As such, I tell them I'm great—that I've gotten a full night's sleep, meditated and worked out, and had a protein shake. Usually it's the truth, but even if it isn't,

> **It's your responsibility to ensure your guests enjoy a perfectly pristine, well-orchestrated, stress-free experience. For them, you must put on a show.**

they would never know the difference. Why? I know that that day is one of the most important in their life, and that I must do my job to the best of my ability. **I don't have the luxury of treating patients poorly one day and doing a terrific job the next. If I make a mistake during surgery, it's a lifelong mistake.**

Myron taught his staff members that to perform, we had to fully inhabit our role as health-care providers who made people feel comfortable. That role left no room for our personal problems or the details of our lives outside that building; such things certainly weren't appropriate topics to discuss with patients. In Myron's office, we were the best possible version of ourselves. We were always stage-ready. Being onstage was something with which I have always been very comfortable.

I come from a theatrical, dramatic Jewish family. My first cousin Ricky Michel has been entertaining audiences in Las Vegas for more than forty years with spot-on impersonations of Frank Sinatra and Dean Martin. Over the course of his career, he has performed in almost every hotel on the strip. Today, at the age of sixty-seven, he's still at it—delighting octogenarians in Florida and throughout the world. My nephew and godson, Jonathan Chase—born Jonathan Greenfield—has been a successful commercial and television actor for nearly fifteen years.

I too had the acting bug, performing in high school plays. I was president of the student council as well and began every day of my senior year by delivering the school morning announcements. I loved it. And as a young kid, I dreamed about being a musician—playing the piano on grand stages around the world.

But like many Jewish mothers, mine believed there were only two acceptable career paths: law and medicine. When I told her about my desire to be a concert pianist, she assured me that if I followed that dream, I'd find myself on a different kind of stage than the one I imagined. Namely, the lobby of the Manhattan Savings Bank on the corner of 86th and Third, from noon to 2 P.M. "I'm sure the little blue-haired ladies will be moved by your performance," she added. She was not far off. My only steady performance work was playing piano at the Jewish Home for the Elderly in Bridgeport, Connecticut, on Monday evenings.

In Myron's office, and to this day, I put my passion to work. Like anyone, I have days when I'm not in a great mood, but at work it's always showtime. **If physicians and dentists are to treat patients effectively, we must be *on* whenever we walk into the room.** It's not about maintaining a facade; it's about forming human connections—the value of which is impossible to overstate.

The Gift of Great Service

My practice partner and I have worked with the Cain and Watters accounting and management firm for the past decade. The office is in Plano, Texas, more than sixteen hundred miles from our practice. Each January, we fly to Texas for an eight-hour meeting. It is not inexpensive, nor is it convenient. Why do we do it? We do it for the same reasons that many of our patients travel tremendous distances to seek our care. They have provided our team with a service that has been unparalleled in terms of its value.

The firm's founder, Darrel Cain, says, "**You have to care more about the value of the service you provide than the**

money you receive." Because the members of his company live out this motto, we continue to work with his firm. We value the service we receive. It is a gift to us.

We strive to offer that same gift to our patients—the gift of service. Each morning, on my way into the office, I say this prayer: "Let me be of service to my team and patients. Please help me be the gift."

After I finish my prayer, I open the door to my conference room where we have our daily morning meeting and say, "It's showtime!" quietly to myself. That ritual helps me set the tone for my team—to truly be the gift my colleagues and patients need.

Props that Create Barriers and Encounters that Break Them Down

In any performance, props play an important role. In my role as a dentist, I want any props I use to strengthen the connection between my patients and my practice. I want the props in our office—the décor, the music, the refreshments—to set the scene and make people feel comfortable.

Some props, however, become barriers to connection between health-care providers and patients. The title of *doctor* sets the health-care provider apart, as does the white coat that so many professionals wear on the job. Those props—the title, the garb—create a distinction between doctor and patient, and they can help or hurt.

Some patients appreciate the pains we take to set ourselves apart. It gives them a sense of comfort and confidence that they're in the care of someone with knowledge and experience. Others just see it as a roadblock to honest communication, one of many in dentistry and medicine today.

White coat syndrome is a real thing and could perhaps be avoided entirely. We don't actually need the wardrobe addition. The white coat doesn't provide the protection of a construction worker's hard hat, for example. If anything, it's an occupational hazard, acting as a potential source of contamination and readily displaying stains—from blood to mustard. Maybe that's a prop that could be left backstage.

Breaking down the barriers between doctors and patients can be challenging today. The kindly old doctor—like television's *Marcus Welby, M.D.*, who cared so much about his patients that he would leave his home and family in the middle of the night to make house calls—has gone the way of the rooftop antenna, mimeograph machine, and rotary telephone.

Rather than sole proprietors focused on delivering comfort, many physicians and dentists have become part of a corporate health care system. Profit drives corporations, and employees often end up taking on the same mentality.

But when doctors my age—I'm sixty-eight as of this writing—went into the field, we did it because we enjoyed helping people. Most of us weren't thinking about money but about doing good. That shift in priorities has led to a lot of dissatisfaction and burnout. In fact, **one Mayo Clinic study found that more than half of physicians experienced at least one symptom of burnout, along with declining rates of work–life balance and satisfaction.**[2] And as you might imagine, burnout and lack of satisfaction are fueled by the sense that doctors can't have the same relationships with patients they once did, due in large part to another ever-present third party: insurance companies (more on this in Chapter 5). **The simple truth is that a health care system based on financial remuneration doesn't serve patients or providers in the end.**

Our current system doesn't treat patients as human beings. At the end of the day, however, that's all people want. They want to feel cared for and loved. They want to make connections. They want to have some certainty about their outcome. The last thing anyone wants is to be a number. More often than not, however, doctors and dentists refer to patients as "the gallbladder in Room 314," or "the root canal in Room 5."

It doesn't have to be that way—and it shouldn't.

The Rest of the Story

Myron taught me that, first and foremost, patients need to know their doctors care for them, that they matter. He did that with every interaction and with the care he took to make sure the waiting room was always stocked with fresh fruit, coffee, and a bottle of chilled white wine—something you certainly wouldn't find in any dental or medical office today.

He had something else you wouldn't find in a dental office nowadays: a German shepherd. The dog would roam the office in a red bandanna, greeting anyone who walked through the door with a polite sniff. His presence significantly reduced the tension in the waiting room.

Although certain aspects of Myron's practice wouldn't fly today, the whole scene provided something that is hard to come by in the medical and dental professions but is extraordinarily important: hospitality. Like Danny Meyer, he understood how to make people feel that he was on their side.

I didn't work with Myron for long. As he got healthier and began taking on more cases, it became clear that the practice wasn't big enough for two dentists. By then, I had already gotten into a periodontal residency program at Emory University in Atlanta. But I never forgot Myron or the lessons he taught me. He helped shape the way I run my practice today. Not long ago, my own office staff gave me a gift: an apple—like the Big Apple—with the word *Showtime* inscribed beneath it. It is a testament to the value our entire team places on showtime, in service.

Despite all Myron taught me, we didn't do much to keep in touch. He was ten years older than me, and I was just a kid when we met. I went on to develop my own practice and became well known in my field. I've taught young dentists at New York University and often give lectures to health-care practitioners around the world. After one such lecture, Myron walked up to me. "Mike," he said, "I'm really proud of you."

Sharing the Power of Showtime

A number of years later, I was standing in the lobby at New York University College of Dentistry between classes when a young guy ambled up to me. "Are you Dr. Sonick?" he asked.

"I am," I said.

"I'm Sivan Finkel." Sure enough, he was the spitting image of Myron—only taller and a little better looking. He was studying to become a dentist, like his dad.

"Not a day goes by that I don't think about your father," I told him. "He taught me all about showtime."

Then, Sivan asked a question that blew me away. "What's showtime?"

Right there, in the Larry Rosenthal Institute at NYU, I began my second lecture of the day—this one impromptu.

In that moment, I decided Myron had to know about the impact he'd had on me and how much the education he provided on showtime had shaped my career. When I got home that night, I picked up a copy of *Implant Site Development*[3], the textbook I had written with Dr. Debby Hwang-my previous practice partner, friend, and frequent collaborator-off the shelf. In it, I wrote an inscription to Myron. I wrote that I think about him every day. I wrote that he taught me how to truly be there for my patients. I wrote that, because of his lessons, I know that no one wants to come see me because I'm a dentist; they want to come to my office because I care.

A lifetime of experience—both professionally and personally—has reinforced what I learned about caring for people from two individuals who are exceptional at it: Myron Finkel and Danny Meyer. **When we run our practices the right way—providing patients with the hospitality and sense of connection they expect from so many other service industries—we better meet their needs, are more financially solvent, and we derive more satisfaction from our work.** Put simply, it's a recipe for success.

But you won't find any recipes here. Instead, you'll find stories—the kind I tell my closest friends, colleagues, and occasionally a lecture room full of young dentists. Each one illustrates why **a focus on hospitality and human connection is vital to the highest quality health care experiences for practitioners and patients alike**. They provide lessons on where we've gone wrong and how to make it right. Consider this book a trusted companion for anyone who provides or receives health care—in short, for all of us.

And like many good stories, it starts at the beginning—mine, that is.

Summary: You're Always on Stage

In the hospitality industry, what matters most is how you make people feel. That's true in medicine and dentistry on multiple levels. Dr. Myron Finkel was an expert in providing patients with a perfectly orchestrated experience—from the beverages he served in the waiting area to his exceptional dental work to his reassuring bedside manner. In his office, it was always showtime.

To be an effective provider, you must take a similar approach. Your training—past and ongoing—serves as your rehearsal. Any personal tasks, from eating your lunch to coordinating childcare to managing a headache, must happen backstage. **Your patients have come for one thing and one thing only, and it's your responsibility to assuage their fears and provide them with the seamless performance they are expecting. That's how you form the human connections we're all seeking.**

Although there can be barriers to forming those connections, from wearing a white coat to the letters after your name and the systems in which you participate, it's up to you to be the gift they need. When you are, you'll find your work to be more fulfilling in every way, shape, and form. This book will give you the tools to do just that.

The Benefits of Putting on a Show

- Providing patients with a showtime-style experience from the moment they step through your doors will put them at ease and make them feel more comfortable.

- Remembering that your office is a stage—and that everything that happens there must be seamless and well-orchestrated—will help you provide a consistently exceptional experience to everyone you serve, something doctors and dentists can't afford *not* to do.

- Presentation matters. When you coordinate every aspect of your performance to convey to your patients that they are receiving the best possible care, they'll see it that way too.

- By maintaining high standards, you also ensure your own integrity—a priceless benefit to you both personally and professionally.

Questions to Consider

As you consider the performance your patients experience, ask yourself the following questions:

- What do people see when they come to my office? What adjustments should I make to provide them with a Broadway-worthy performance every time they visit?

- Are there external conditions I should consider in crafting my office environment and the performance patients experience? (For example, COVID-19 required me to reconsider my scheduling and intake process while maintaining as much of a sense of normalcy as possible.)

- Does the current show I'm putting on undermine the clinical care I provide in any way? For example, would my patients appreciate me ditching the white coat, or would they actually prefer me to go out of my way to highlight my training and professional experience?

- Do I embrace being onstage and performing, or do I need support in this area? If so, are there individuals or organizations with whom I could connect to hone this skill?

- Do I make sure that the patient always comes first, no matter what?

- Have I ever let my personal feelings or mood undermine my connection with a patient or team members? What might I do differently in the future to ensure that this does not occur?

2

Blood on the Pavement

My Story as a Dentist and a Patient

For a fraction of a second, I floated in midair, my stomach dropping before the rest of me did. The moment of flight was short-lived, though: my face hit the ground, what felt like teeth-first. Think of matzo—that dry Passover cracker—crumbling against pavement, but with all the blood of the first plague.

When I came to, that was the first thing I saw-blood everywhere, on my hands, my shirt, the ground. I felt it spreading across my face, stickily coating my chin. My mother was hovering over me, sure I was dead. She was shrieking, but everything seemed oddly quiet, as if someone had pushed a button and sent time and space into slow motion.

Out of the corner of my eye, I could see Paul's bike. The handlebars—which I had flown over—rested against the ground.

Paul Balsano was my next-door neighbor. He always had the coolest stuff, and that included a banana seat bike, complete with high handlebars and chrome fenders. He had generously let me borrow it during one 1960s summer in Bridgeport, Connecticut. As I had flown down the street with the wind in my hair, his dog, Tippy, jumped on me—at least I think he did. My memories from that day start with me going airborne before breaking my fall with my face.

When I clambered to my feet, I saw my two front teeth sitting there, blood-streaked and glistening, on the sidewalk. I tongued the ragged edges of what remained: short stumps where my permanent teeth had been. I was eight years old, and those two teeth had just come in.

My mother collected herself, scooped up me and the teeth, and drove us all to see Dr. Marvin Aaronson, an oral surgeon in downtown Bridgeport. Back then, dentistry wasn't what it is today, and I was fortunate that Dr. Aaronson was both close and capable. He put arch bars in my mouth to stabilize my teeth and wired shut my jaw, which had been broken during the fall.

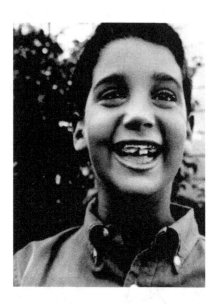

For the next eight weeks, I couldn't eat solid food. Everything I consumed—meat, potatoes, and more—went through a Waring® blender (the first version of the Cuisinart®) and then into my mouth through a straw.

When the arch bars came off at summer's end, I needed root canals on the two front teeth. In 1961, only two endodontists (dentists that performed root canals) practiced in Connecticut: one in Stamford and one in Hartford. I saw Dr. Phil Levin in Stamford; he did two excellent root canals, one of which remains in my mouth to this day—sixty years later.

Though I was lucky enough to have a great oral surgeon and endodontist, they could only do so much for me cosmetically. My doctors didn't want to crown my teeth until I stopped growing, so I went through grammar and high school with two brown stubs for front teeth. My sister, Kathi, dubbed me "Broken Teeth," an unfortunate nickname that stuck. Worse, my family and friends quickly labeled me as accident-prone.

In addition to commenting on my clumsiness, my dad would often tell me I just wasn't good with my hands. He himself was a talented carpenter and engineer. He was a big, powerful man, and the world seemed to respect his confident hands. He was the strongest man I knew—both physically and mentally. He challenged me to be the best version of myself, to always work harder. As a young boy, I felt diminutive and overwhelmed in his powerful presence. He had a very different childhood than I did. Despite our outward differences, he became not only my greatest teacher but my role model.

A Tough-Guy Cinderella Story

My father had a difficult childhood—a literal Cinderella story. His mother died when he was four. Unable to shoulder the burden himself, my newly widowed grandfather asked the neighbors to raise my father instead. They agreed to take him in, but they certainly didn't treat him as their own. When the family went out for a Sunday drive, they didn't invite my father to join them. Instead, they left him at home with instructions to shovel coal in the basement.

The family provided him with the bare minimum, and eyeglasses weren't on the list. With bad eyes and no money of his own, he was a straight-C student throughout his primary school career. At sixteen, he got a job at a local grocery store and made enough money to buy his own glasses. Finally able to see, he improved his grades, and he got into Northeastern

University with a partial scholarship. He began studying engineering.

One day in class, he jotted down a date a year in the future—January 15, 1943—along with what would turn out to be an accurate prophecy: wounded left leg, Luxembourg.

A year later, that's exactly where he ended up: in Luxembourg with a wounded leg. After being drafted into World War II, he had taken a piece of shrapnel in battle. He recovered in a Paris hospital and spent a few years in France before returning to the United States at age twenty-two.

During his time away, he grew bigger, stronger, and more confident. What he hadn't gained during his time abroad, though, was a college degree. He had always wanted to be a dentist, and thanks to the tuition benefits of the GI Bill, he could afford to pursue that goal. However, at twenty-two, he didn't think he could afford to be in school for another handful of years—he figured by the time he graduated, he'd be much too old to start a family. So he completed his undergraduate degree in engineering at the University of Bridgeport in Connecticut (where he met my mom, Joanne Berman) and then went on to work at Sikorsky Aircraft.

Lessons Learned

My father knew how to use his hands to build things. When I was a kid, he kept a full set of power tools in the basement—saws, drill presses, and joiners—tools he never allowed me to touch. Instead, I'd watch him work, carry things from the basement to the garage for him, stack bricks (being extra careful not to jam my fingers), and get him lunch. But the tools were off-limits. After my accident, my mother became overprotective. She didn't want me to do anything where I could hurt myself. My father followed her lead, attempting to keep me away from anything sharp, heavy, or motorized. Even scissors were off-limits to me as a kid.

Of course, making those power tools off-limits didn't stop me from having sledding accidents that resulted in stitches in my hands. Nor did it keep me from chipping another tooth or from falling off two more bikes. And all that overprotection failed when I broke my ankle while playing outside.

When I hurt my ankle, my dad assured me it was just a sprain and instructed me to stand in the snow to ice it down. "It's good for it," he said, as he left me standing knee-deep in powder in front of our house and closed the door behind him.

My father had a couple of mantras that reinforced his tough-guy approach. One was "Hard work never killed anybody." Another was "I feel no pain." I repeated the latter as I stood there, barefoot, unsure of which hurt more: the freezing snow against my skin or the radiating pain deep inside my ankle. The next day, I went to the hospital. The x-rays proved him wrong: it wasn't just a sprain. I had broken my ankle.

Consciously or not, I set out to be like my father. I wanted to be strong, fearless, and hardworking. When I was a young boy, he handed me a small white plaque with the words, "One man with courage makes a majority." That sign hung on the back of my bedroom door my entire childhood. He told me it was true, and I believed him.

His nurturing skills may have been lacking, but I learned from him how to persist. Combining his tough-guy approach to life with my genetic disposition determined the shape of my life and helped make me a contrarian. If you tell me to go left, chances are I'll go right. If you say it is impossible, I'm doing it.

Don't Accept the Status Quo

My tendency to question authority has served me well. I don't accept the status quo or take anyone's word for it—you've got to prove to me that your way is the right one. When I was a dental student, teachers told me to do things a certain way. I have always believed that a good student challenges the teacher to prove that the method they're teaching is, in fact, the best approach. Often, students learn subpar strategies, in part because they're so willing to accept a superior's word as gospel. Instead, students should do what they believe is right, based on literature and proven experience—not just what they're told.

Eventually, I would show my father that I *was* good with my hands—and that I could fulfill the dream he'd always had.

And if my dad's desire to become a dentist planted the seed in my mind, my extensive experiences in the dentist's chair as a kid, both good and bad, served as fertilizer.

Unlike the oral surgeon and endodontist I had seen after my first bike accident, my childhood dentist didn't leave a good taste in my mouth. My penchant for candy, combined with my dentist's overzealous approach, meant a number of new fillings every year.

Summer after summer, I sat for hours in his home office as he drilled into my teeth without anesthetic, the smell of tooth dust—like burnt feathers—emanating from my mouth and filling the air. There I'd be, trapped, looking back and forth between the tray of sharp picks and probes to my right and the drill with its spinning cord hovering over me as my dentist yelled at his wife and kids through the wall. Hard to believe, but he left a lit cigarette burning in the dental lab. During short breaks he would go to the lab, take a drag, and go back to working on my teeth. This was before the advent of personal protective equipment (PPE), and he did not wear gloves. His yellow nicotine- and tar-stained fingers were clearly visible as he worked in my mouth. Needless to say, it wasn't he who inspired me to go into the profession.

In 1970, when I was about to graduate from high school, he recommended crowns with posts in them—two little rods that would go down the middle of my teeth.

After what felt like a lifetime of having my mouth worked on, I told him I didn't want them.

"Why not?" he asked. "They make the teeth stronger."

I wasn't a dentist at the time, of course, but that just didn't make sense to me. It seemed to me that they would fracture the teeth I had. It was my own prophetic moment; today we know that posts can contribute to the fracture of teeth. I only recommend them when absolutely necessary, not as an automatic response to a root canal.

Meanwhile, the good experiences—the moments of true connection with physicians and dentists—encouraged me to practice dentistry myself. My orthodontist, Dr. Ernest Mendeloff, ran a beautiful office in a charming old house on a tree-lined street in Bridgeport, Connecticut. The radio was always set to classical music, and when a commercial came on, his nurses—all of whom seemed to be from Sweden and dressed pristinely in perfect white clogs—would click a button to silence the noise.

He was always professional and put together, a string tie peeking out from beneath his white coat. He was generous too—so generous that he once offered to have me live in his house after I finished dental school. That was just the type of guy he was. He thrived on connection.

My personal dental history played in the back of my mind during my time at Colgate University in Hamilton, New York, where I was a predental student with an English minor. Filled with kids from the Northeast, for me, my undergraduate experience felt like little more than an extension of high school. Although the school was beautiful and I got an excellent academic education, with its homogenous student body, my time at Colgate didn't teach me much about people.

Dental school provided a more stimulating environment. I went to the University of Connecticut School of Dental Medicine, not because it was the best dental school in the country—although at the time, it might have been—but because it was $900 a year. Tuition at the private schools I had gotten into was at least $20,000. I was footing the bill myself, which made the University of Connecticut quite appealing. Unbeknownst to me, I would wind up getting a phenomenal education at a very reasonable cost.

I moved in with a high school friend, Barry Messinger—who's now an orthopedic surgeon—and his college roommate from Yale, Bill Cappiello—who became a sports medicine doctor in California. We found an inexpensive garden basement apartment in New Britain and lived together for four years. In the 1970s, medical trainees were much more idealistic. Although I was concerned with the cost of tuition, my friends and I weren't thinking about the money we would make as doctors. We just loved medicine and the idea of being able to help people. This shared sense of values has kept us close for over forty years.

Treat the Whole Person

It was 1975, and Harald Löe, a Norwegian periodontist, was dean of the University of Connecticut School of Dental Medicine. Ten years earlier, he had published the seminal paper in the field: "Experimental Gingivitis in Man[4]." It was the first paper to show that when people don't brush their teeth, gingivitis develops—their gums bleed.

He conducted an experiment, asking twenty-one Norwegian dental students not to brush for twenty-one days. At the beginning of the experiment, all of them had perfectly healthy gums. Within seven to nine days, all of their gums were bleeding. He instructed them to resume brushing. Ten days later, the bleeding stopped. For the first time, Harald Löe demonstrated that gingivitis is not only preventable by brushing but also that it is reversable.

Dr. Löe also cultured plaque from dental students' gums each day, examining the bacterial profile throughout the experiment. He noted the changes: harmful bacteria replaced healthy bacteria over the first seven to nine days. This corresponded to an increase in bleeding of the gums. When the students reinstated the use of toothbrushes, healthy bacteria flourished once again. **Dr. Löe was the first to correlate the clinical symptoms of disease and of health with the type of bacteria that were present. It's hard to believe that this revelation did not take place until 1965.**

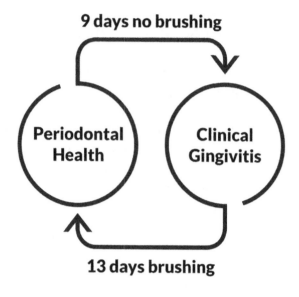

9 days no brushing

Periodontal
Health

Clinical
Gingivitis

13 days brushing

Harald Löe
Dean, UCONN, 1979

On my first day of dental school, I didn't know I was going to become a periodontist. I didn't know who Harald Löe was; almost nobody did back then. I didn't know about his historic experiment, either. But from the moment he addressed our class, I knew he was special. For one thing, he called us *doctors* from the get-go.

"You are not just dentists," he said. "You are doctors. Physicians of the oral cavity. In Europe, dentistry is a subspecialty of medicine, and because of that, you will take care of the whole body as well."

At the time, the University of Connecticut, like Harvard, was one of the few schools in the country that required dental students to go through two years of medical school to enter their third year. We had to pass Part I of the medical boards to progress, all while completing our dental training. The members of my class went to school six days a week for two years. It was hard, but I loved it. I made some of the best friends of my life during that program—dentists and physicians who still come together on Block Island each year to revel in the unique connection forged by what we went through. We had each other, and we had Harald Löe as our leader. Under his tutelage, we didn't just learn to do crowns or extract teeth; we learned to take care of people.

Other dental programs required students to complete a number of procedures to graduate: twenty crowns, fifteen extractions, three dentures, two fillings, and so on. It didn't matter who the patient was; you just had to get the total amount of required work done. If you needed only four fillings to graduate, but the patient needed four fillings, two crowns, and an extraction, you could do your fillings and move on, passing the patient to someone else. I felt this was detrimental to the patient and demeaning to the process— patients passed and traded like baseball cards.

Fortunately, the University of Connecticut took a different approach. You had to do everything the patient needed. Dr. Löe taught us that the first order of business was to control the patient's pain, then control infection. We couldn't move on to other procedures until we completed those steps. We called our periodontal clinic "the periodontal hotel," the joke being that once you checked in, you never checked out. If you couldn't motivate your patients to brush and floss and get their plaque score (the number of bacteria left on the teeth) down to 10 percent, you couldn't do the restorative treatment you needed to finish the program. I did not know it at the time, but the patient's level of home care and oral hygiene were among the most important determinants of success and long-term dental and oral health.

The Order of Treatment

1. Emergency Care
2. Treatment of Active Disease
3. Functional Rehabilitation
4. Esthetics
5. Maintenance

As a result of this policy, we couldn't do as many procedures as others did, because we had to finish the course of treatment for one patient before moving on to the next. Very few schools, even today, provide an experience rooted in philosophy, science, diagnosis, treatment planning, and proper examination. Few programs provide much insight on how to treat the whole person, on how to be physicians of the oral cavity. There's not a day when I don't think of Harold Löe and all he taught me—including the importance of treating the whole person, not just the tooth. He was the first dentist to show me the immense value of viewing patients as people, not procedures.

A Lifetime of Learning—Personally and Professionally

Graduation from dental school didn't mark the end of my learning or my personal experience with dentistry. In my forties, the temporomandibular joint (TMJ) issue I'd had for years—clenching and grinding my teeth—resulted not only in significant tooth wear (attrition), but also in tooth fractures.

The less-than-ideal dentistry from my childhood led to a bad bite, which contributed to all that clenching and grinding and pain. Back during my residency at Emory University in Atlanta, I used to take ibuprofen before my shift in the TMJ and facial pain clinic because just listening to patients talk about their pain would trigger my own. I eventually ground away over 50 percent of my teeth. Carole, my wife, affectionately referred to me as "Little Teeth."

The year I turned forty-six, I fractured five back teeth, which required temporary crowns, throwing off my bite even further and leading to more pain. It seemed anything and everything could set it off. If I saw someone experience jaw pain on television or in a movie, my own jaw would start to throb. I tried not to talk about it to avoid triggering it. My jaw became so temperamental, the ache so overwhelming, that when patients came in with TMJ-related jaw pain, I immediately referred them to other dentists since it literally hurt to hear their stories.

That year, I went to see my friend Dr. Steve Rothenberg, a prosthodontist in Darien, Connecticut. I had been working with him my entire career and considered him to be not only an excellent clinician but also a thoughtful and comprehensive practitioner who had a heart of gold. His philosophy of care was congruent with my own. I told him about the fractures and the pain and asked what he thought I should do. He made models of my mouth and we looked at them together. We weighed the pros and cons of the various forms of treatment out there. We considered implants, which were becoming quite popular then. Implants are a great replacement for teeth, but I knew they wouldn't necessarily be better than my own.

We decided to crown the teeth I had—twenty-three in total, including the front teeth I had fractured when I was eight—to give me an ideal bite. In the process, we found that one of the original teeth fractured in my bike accident had split and needed to be removed and replaced with a bridge.

This full-mouth rehabilitation required four-hour visits a few times a month for about six months. As much as hearing about my patients' jaw pain bothered me, I've always been a pretty easygoing dental patient. I felt calm and confident throughout the process, in part because I trusted Steve so much. He's one of the kindest, most competent doctors I know.

Most patients don't trust dentists that easily. I trusted Steve not only because we had been friends since my first year in practice but also because I had seen and understood his work. Plus, I had gotten to know many of his patients quite well as we worked together on numerous full-mouth rehabilitations. They were uniform in their love for him as a human being because they always felt so well cared for.

It's been more than twenty years since I had all my teeth crowned. For two decades, I've been pain-free, and I haven't had any additional dentistry outside of getting my teeth cleaned every three months and regular brushing and flossing. It's not because I have built a perfect lifestyle in adulthood, free of sugar and acidic foods. In all likelihood, I was overtreated as a child—I probably didn't need all those fillings. More than that, maintenance goes a long way, and I haven't missed a cleaning in twenty years.

Now I have a smile I feel good about. But for most of my life, I wasn't proud of my teeth. For years, my mouth was a source of discomfort both physically and emotionally. I eventually realized that sharing my story could have a significant, positive impact on my patients.

The Power of Sharing Your Story

I have plenty of opportunities to hear from patients about their pain and self-consciousness about their teeth. One day,

I listened as a patient complained to me about all the ways she thought her mouth had betrayed her.

When she finished speaking, I said, "You know, I'd trade mouths with you."

"Yeah?" she replied, unconvinced. "You have beautiful teeth."

"I have beautiful teeth?" I repeated.

"Yes, you've got a great smile," she said.

"It's all fake," I told her. "The only plastic surgery I've had."

"What are you talking about?"

"Look," I said, opening my mouth. I pointed at the four gold crowns toward the back, where I had fractured my teeth from that clenching and grinding. I had chosen gold because it's one of the best materials you can put in your mouth. While it might not be the most cosmetically appealing choice—unless you're Mike Tyson, that is—gold crowns can withstand the tremendous amount of force those back teeth take, and they are more resistant to decay than conventional porcelain crowns. The crowns also served as visible evidence of what my mouth had been through.

"Wow," she said.

I nodded. "I have twenty-three crowns. I've lost nine teeth, including the front two when I was eight."

"What happened?" she asked.

"Bike accident."

Her eyes began to well up. I could tell she was picturing that eight-year-old boy, scared and bleeding on the sidewalk.

"It's been a long time," I reassured her, "about fifty-five years. The little boy was okay in the end." But in that moment, she was back there, with him. My experience resonated with her. Knowing that I could relate to her—because my mouth had actually been worse than hers—allowed her to put her trust in me.

Trust is a very big deal. Building relationships with patients is all about establishing trust. One of the most effective ways to do that is to know when—and how—to share a story. It's not always helpful or appropriate to share your personal experience, but when it's done right, it can prove invaluable to your patients.

Trust is a very big deal.

For many years, I didn't realize the importance of my own story. But when I told it for the first time, a light bulb came on. When I talk to my patients about my dental care, they understand that not only do I know how to fix them but also that I *was* them—or worse.

Today, there's not a new patient to whom I don't tell the story. Like my full-mouth rehabilitation and the end of my pain, it took a while to get there. I practiced for twenty-five years before I began telling patients about my personal experience with dentistry—about the accident I had when I was a kid, about the nine teeth I lost, about the time, effort, and decision-making it took to fix it all. But now I realize that it has the potential to show them the value of quality treatment and to let them know that if they're suffering, it gets better—I'm proof.

Sharing your story is key. It's essential to one of the most important tenets of success in any field: connection. That kind of connection is at the heart of so many programs. Alcoholics Anonymous is predicated on the concept that only recovering alcoholics—those who have been there—can help others get sober. The same is true for Weight Watchers. There's a reason people with model-perfect bodies who have never struggled with their weight don't lead those groups. We all find comfort in knowing someone has overcome the same obstacles we're facing.

I had the opportunity to teach this lesson to one of my practice partners, who I will call Dr. John. He grew up in a small town in rural China. He spent time in his family's private dental practice, his destiny to become a fourth-generation dentist from the time he was in diapers. He came to the United States at age twenty to pursue his undergraduate degree at the State University of New York at Albany, where he majored in chemistry and was valedictorian of his class. He completed his dental education at Tufts University in Boston and went on to specialize in periodontics under the tutelage of Dr. Vincent Iancono at Stony Brook University. Despite his exceptional education and a lifetime spent around dentistry, he was struggling when he joined my practice.

> **Sharing your story is key. It's essential to one of the most important tenets of success in any field: connection.**

First, he was young. He wanted to be a successful, respected doctor, but that's hard to do when you're thirty-two and you walk into a practice that has been established for as long as you've been alive.

He also had some cultural barriers to overcome. All that time studying and working to advance his career hadn't left much opportunity to absorb the culture of the Northeast. And there was the rub: that cultural competency was essential to his success.

When he joined my practice, he asked if I would teach him some of the techniques he hadn't learned in his residency.

"I will," I said, "but you have to do something first. Do you like *Seinfeld?*"

"It's okay," he said.

"Well, that's the problem."

"What do you mean?"

"Before you can be a truly great surgeon, you have to be able to relate to your patients. You came here to work with me because I'm well known for what I do. But what I'm most proud of is not the surgical techniques I've perfected; it's the relationships I have with my patients. If they didn't relate to me, do you think they'd allow me to do all these surgeries in the first place?"

He cocked his head, listening.

"We're in the Northeast," I continued. "In the Northeast, we say what's on our mind. We're blunt. The culture of our practice is similar to *Seinfeld*'s. Watching will teach you how to relate to our patients. So, here's the deal. I'll teach you some advanced surgical techniques, but not until you watch all 180 episodes of *Seinfeld*."

"Really?" he asked.

"Yup," I said.

That night, he watched the first two episodes.

"What did you think?" I asked.

"It was okay," he said, with a shrug.

Around episode seven, he told me he was starting to like it.

"Keep watching," I said.

Being the diligent student he is, he finished all 180 episodes.

"Will you teach me now?" he asked.

"Yes," I replied, "but there's an advanced course."

"What's that?" he asked.

"Larry David," I said, joking.

Beyond his ongoing cultural education, though, Dr. John needed a story. When he started working with me, he didn't think he had one. He used to talk to patients about dentistry. He'd talk to them about pocket depth, about bleeding, about pus. He would refer to their missing teeth as numbers—overlooking the embarrassment the gaps in patients' smiles caused them in the process. He didn't understand that the words and phrases he used—cementum, loss of attachment, mucogingival defects, malocclusion, osseointegration, calculus: vocabulary straight out of a dentistry textbook—didn't mean anything to the person sitting in the chair in front of him. Instead, those words, foreign and sharp-edged, scared them.

He didn't realize the truth in that adage, attributed to former President Theodore Roosevelt, "People don't care how much you know until they know how much you care." In his quest to provide an abundance of information, Dr. John was failing to cultivate and convey something far more important: trust.

No one knows the value of trust more than Todd Williams, Vice President of Culture Development for Centura Health, with a twenty-year tenure developing and implementing service delivery for Four Seasons Hotels and Resorts. I had the pleasure of meeting Todd at a speakers' conference in Kansas City. Listening to him for just a few minutes, I felt as though I had found my soulmate for customer service in health care. I was so moved by the passion of his message that I invited him to speak at the Fairfield County Dental Club (FCDC), our continuing education society in Connecticut. At the FCDC meeting, he shared that patients are vulnerable and need to know that they are in a good place. In a sense, when they are in your chair or on your table or in your medical office, they are like children— they worry and need someone to care for them. They want to hear that it will be okay. The right story can convey compassion and care and can reassure them.

Dr. John is a scientist by nature, a born technician. I call him a professional golfer. When he tees up the ball and takes a swing, all he sees is that ball. His nature made him a great surgeon in terms of technique and attention to detail, but it didn't do him any favors in terms of getting patients to relate to him. As a result, his case closure rate—the percentage of patients who would say yes to treatment—hovered around 30 or 40 percent. In a healthy practice, that rate should be 80 to 90 percent.

I knew I had to start a different conversation with him to help him take a different tack with patients. "Why did you become a dentist?" I asked him.

He began telling me about where he had come from and what he had been through. First, it was the basics—the stuff I already knew. With some prodding, he started to go deeper. He didn't become a dentist because his mom was one or because he had grown up watching his grandmother in that family practice. He became a dentist because he had had periodontal disease himself. He had been through periodontal treatment, and he wanted to be able to provide patients with a positive, pain-free experience. Today, that's the story he shares. And his case acceptance rate is the same as mine: 90 percent.

Each of us has a different story to tell, but we relate to each other in the same way. Everyone wants transparency, openness, respect, and a personalized approach. People want to know you care.

I'm not an extrovert by any means. I don't enjoy chatting with the Starbucks barista about the weather. I don't feel compelled to talk to the acquaintance I inevitably meet there about their shoes or the kind of car they drive or their latest vacation or how their investments are doing. I don't care about professional or college sports. I do, however, appreciate the power of a meaningful conversation.

What do I care about, if it's not money or sports or cars? I care about what you care about. What makes you tick? What keeps you up at night? What moves you most?

Nineteenth-century historian Henry Thomas Buckle said, "Men and women range themselves into three classes or orders of intelligence; you can tell the lowest class by their habit of always talking about persons; the next by the fact that their habit is always to converse about things; the highest by their preference for the discussion of ideas[5]." Some version of that observation has since been attributed to numerous people, including First Lady Eleanor Roosevelt. The concept has endured because it's true.

Buckle and the others who have made this their mantra are right. It's ideas that have real value. Most people don't go there; they distract themselves with gossip or what's on TV. In the process, they sacrifice the opportunity to forge deep connections.

To create those bonds, you have to move beyond gossip, beyond current events, even beyond the basic getting-to-know-you questions on which so many dentists rely. I know practitioners who ask each patient the same five questions, dutifully jotting down their answers in the chart so they can follow up the next time they come in. That only leads to stilted conversations. It won't make you a good dentist or physician.

What will? Getting to the heart of the matter. Doing the right thing for the right reasons. Finding their *why*—and yours. We'll go there next. But I'll give you a hint: it's not the money.

Summary: Sharing Stories That Matter to Your Patients

Reading this chapter, you may have wondered why I took the time to tell you my story. To be honest, I wasn't sure how much to share. But chances are, as the chapter unfolded, you began to understand who I am, why I became a dentist, and even why I decided to write this book. Our stories tell others so much about why we do what we do (more on that *why* later).

You also may have discovered commonalities between our experiences. Perhaps you went into medicine or dentistry for the same reasons I did. Maybe a traumatic event at a pivotal point in your life has driven your decisions in one direction or another. Maybe our backgrounds are similar. Those connections have value. And that's why having a story is such an important tool when it comes to building trust with your patients.

Of course, you must use your judgment. Oversharing is neither appropriate nor helpful. But a carefully deployed story, one that highlights where you've been—and even why you're uniquely qualified to do the work you do—can do wonders for patient–provider relationships.

If you're not sure where to start, think about the ways in which I counseled Dr. John. Like mine, his story lay in why he decided to become a dentist—including not only his family history but also the periodontal disease and treatment he experienced at an early age. When he shared with patients what he had been through and why he wanted to help, his acceptance rate skyrocketed. Why? Because the connections built with those patients through his story were based on something deeper than technical terms or even skill: humanity.

You may have to dig deeper than you've gone before to unearth the story that matters most, but when you do, you'll know. If you're still unsure about whether you've hit on the right content, test it out. Tell a patient your story and see how they react. If it seems to put them at ease, you're on the right page.

The next step is to ask questions and be an active listener. Inquire about what they like to do, their hobbies and passions, their children, what they enjoy reading, and more.

After all, being a good conversationalist is just about asking questions. You don't have to know everything; people will fill in the gaps for you. Make a note of what they said and refer to it in your next conversation. Patients want to know about you, but they also want to feel heard. Keep in mind, this conversation may not be about dentistry or medicine at all. The goal is to get to know them as a person, not just a patient or procedure.

A Story Can Make All the Difference

- Stories provide patients with insight into how and why you do what you do.

- They establish trust and connection, two essential elements of relationships that cannot be falsified.

- They have the power to comfort and reassure patients that they are making the right choice, particularly when deciding whether a particular course of treatment is the way to go.

- Sharing your story also encourages them to open up, allowing you to further tailor your approach to address their concerns and better meet their needs.

Questions to Consider

As you begin to craft your story, consider the following questions:

- What events in your life have shaped you into the person you have become, both personally and professionally?

- Why do you do what you do? (If you need more help figuring this out, stay tuned—we'll dig deeper into your *why* later.)

- Why do you think long-term patients keep coming back? Does that insight play into your story?

- What do you want those you treat to know?

- How much of who you are do you feel comfortable sharing with patients?

- Do you believe there is strength in vulnerability?

- How can you connect to your patients in a more meaningful way?

3

Setting the Table

The Power of Hospitality

A restaurant called Centro opened up just around the corner from my office about a month after I opened my practice in downtown Fairfield in 1985. In the front window stood a beautiful pasta machine, and you could watch the cooks making fresh pasta as you waited for a table or took an evening stroll through town. It was a remarkably innovative concept in the mid-1980s—a strategic decision that heightened the experience for guests and onlookers alike.

As a new business owner myself, I was intrigued by such a move. I began paying close attention to the restaurant's progress. I also began to think about my own practice and how it—and all dental and medical operations—were more like restaurants than one might think.

Centro is still open today, and that's a big deal. It means the restaurant is doing something right. Many restaurants fail within their first year in business, and many that make it past that challenging milestone often shutter within five years of opening[6]. As of this writing, Centro has been in business for thirty-five years. The restaurant is as busy as ever. The food is good. The experience is as consistent as it is great. Whenever I go to Centro, I know exactly what I'm going to get—and I'm never disappointed.

Today, I have three favorite restaurants, and I've studied the way each runs, looking for insight into how to provide an ideal experience in my own operation. One of these restaurants is Pasta Nostra in Norwalk, Connecticut. It opened in 1984—just a year before my practice. It began as a pasta store and lunch spot. Soon, thanks to owner and chef Joe Bruno's cooking, Pasta Nostra was drawing crowds who'd line up around the block for his fresh pasta and hearty Italian fare, even in the dead of winter. Eventually, the shop began getting attention from the *New York Times* and even Martha Stewart. Today, the restaurant has expanded to include a full bar and dinner service in a hip dining room.

Another favorite is Frasca, which the owner modeled after the friendly informal neighborhoods of northeastern Italy, particularly the sub-alpine region of Friuli-Venezia Giulia. Frasca is in Boulder, Colorado—about two thousand miles from my house—and I've been there at least thirty times. It's just that good.

My youngest daughter, Jenn, and I went out to dinner every Wednesday—just the two of us—for years. One of our local favorites was Pasta Nostra. When we were away from home, I scoured websites to find good restaurants, which is how I found Frasca. Jenn was touring colleges, and we stayed in Boulder, Colorado, one night. We were looking for restaurants in town, and I stumbled upon Frasca's website. It looked good online, so we decided to give it a try.

The restaurant was beautiful—all understated elegance—and the meal was excellent. Afterward, one of the waiters came over to ask how we had enjoyed the experience. He chatted with my daughter, who had been a food runner at the Angus Steakhouse in Fairfield, Connecticut. Before we left, he told me, "If you ever need anything, just give me a call," and handed me his card.

I didn't know it at the time, but that waiter was Bobby Stuckey, the owner of the restaurant and one of just a handful of American Master Sommeliers. Bobby, one of the top restaurateurs in the country, had extended us tremendous hospitality even though we had only been there for one meal.

My daughter ended up attending the University of Colorado, and through the years, we went back to Frasca many times. Bobby always remembered us. I don't drink, and the waitstaff seemed to remember that as well, serving me sparkling water or soda when I arrived. Any time I had trouble getting a reservation, I did what he said and gave him a call.

Like many high-end restaurants, Frasca has one table in the kitchen where you can watch meals being prepared. The kitchen is immaculate, as you might expect, and between each of the two or three seatings they have per night, the team wipes everything down and puts fresh paper on all of the counters. The lucky few seated there will see Stuckey come in and out, meticulously dressed. Each time he passes by, he washes his hands in a sink reserved just for him.

During one meal in that kitchen, Bobby stopped by our table. "Good to see you again," he said, though we hadn't been there in at least four months. "I remember when you were first here," he told us. "You sat at table sixteen." That first visit had been three years prior. We marveled at his memory, and he just smiled.

Later, we learned that he keeps notes of every diner's experience at the restaurant—maintaining computer profiles complete with what each person orders, where they sat, and the dates they were there. That way, anyone on his team can replicate the exceptional experience he provides, whether he's there or not. It is hospitality at its finest, and with Bobby, it extends far beyond the cataloging of details.

Going above and Beyond

When my son graduated from college, he wasn't sure what he wanted to do professionally. I called Bobby, who said he'd be happy to talk to him, and they had a thirty-minute conversation about my son's next move. When we celebrated my daughter's graduation at the restaurant, he gave me a T-shirt. It was simple, all black, with a pig on the front and the word "Scarpetta" on the back. Three years later, I was eating at Le Coucou, a hot new restaurant in New York, and wearing that T-shirt under a sports jacket. "Oh," said the *maître d'*, "you know Bobby Stuckey. He was just here last week."

A few years after that, I was back at Frasca, telling Bobby that story. That night, we ate in the dining room, but I asked him whether I could get a photo in the kitchen. "Sure," he said, and my family and I followed him to the back. He was entirely comfortable bringing anyone there at any point. I feel the same way about my office. It's always pristine, and thus, I never hesitate to invite a patient in. Our insides match our outsides, something we'll talk about in more detail later in Chapter 10. All successful businesses have an underlying commitment to excellence. It is much easier to provide a consistently exceptional customer experience if there is consistency and transparency in all levels of the organization, both inside and outside. A great restaurant is comfortable allowing customers to see their kitchen at any time. The same should be true of a great medical practice. Allowing patients to see what is behind the curtain is a sign of a well-run organization.

At Danny Meyer's restaurant, The Modern at New York's Museum of Modern Art, I had another exceptional experience thanks to Danny's excellent hospitality. The Modern is another extraordinarily beautiful space, overlooking the Abby Aldrich Rockefeller Sculpture Garden.

I wanted to take my staff there for our annual celebration but hadn't been there before. That gave my wife and me an excuse to visit. I told the *maître d'* that I would be coming back with my staff a few months later and asked whether it would be possible for Danny himself to join us. Of course, I didn't expect him to say yes. But he told me I could certainly ask and gave me Danny's secretary's email.

I sent the request and received a prompt response: "Danny is very sorry that he won't be able to make it. He's not going to be in New York that day," it read. Having figured as much, I quickly moved on.

But when I returned with my team that summer, the manager apologized that Danny wasn't able to be there, unprompted. Furthermore, he had something for me: a signed copy of *Setting the Table*. Inside, Danny had written an inscription:

To Michael,

Here's to the power of hospitality in restaurants and in the dental chair.

Enjoy,

Danny Meyer, July 2018

Now, I don't know how many requests Danny gets on a daily basis. But I do know that his hospitality group owns and operates sixteen restaurants as well as 275 Shake Shacks around the world. And I know that acts of kindness like the one he did for me don't affect him from a financial perspective. With a net worth of hundreds of millions, he certainly doesn't need my business. Rather, hospitality is in his DNA. And it is his natural hospitality-driven approach that has enabled him to grow his business from a single restaurant to a billion-dollar operation.

My third favorite restaurant is actually one of Danny Meyer's: Gramercy Tavern in Manhattan. The menu is straightforward and delicious—as comforting as Danny's signature hospitality. With seven James Beard Awards to its name, you've probably at least heard of it even if you haven't made the trek yourself.

What Gets You up in the Morning?

How did Danny Meyer get so good at providing the kind of experiences customers come back for time and again? He grew up around them. When he was young, his father had a career as a successful travel agent with his own travel agency and a small hotel in St. Louis. Danny's parents frequently took him on European vacations, visiting family inns and restaurants along the way. Even as a child, what he saw, tasted, and felt inspired him.

But like me, he felt pressure to pursue one of the two prominent career paths Jewish mothers are well known for pushing on their children: medicine or law. He chose law. The night before the LSAT, he had dinner with an uncle. "I can't believe I'm doing this LSAT thing tomorrow. I don't even want to be a lawyer," he said.

His uncle replied, "So why are you? You know you don't want to be a lawyer. Why don't you just do what you've been thinking about doing your whole life?"

"What's that?" Danny asked.

"What do you mean, 'What's that'? Since you were a child all you've ever talked or thought about is food and restaurants. Why don't you just open a restaurant[7]?"

By now you know the ending to this story: he did just that, many times over. Danny Meyer is one of the most renowned restaurateurs out there. Ultimately, he followed his heart, and it paid off.

Fortunately for me, dentistry did become my passion. I wanted to fulfill my father's dream of being a dentist and prove I was good with my hands, and I learned to love it along the way. But unlike many physicians and dentists, it's not the technical stuff that gets me out of bed in the morning. It's providing patients with an extraordinary experience from beginning to end—an approach modeled not only on what I've learned over more than four decades in the field but also on Danny Meyer and his focus on hospitality. His best-selling book, *Setting the Table: The Transforming Power of Hospitality in Business*—the one he inscribed for me—has long been my bible. Its lessons inspire so much of what I do.

How Do You Make People Feel?

Of course, many books have been written on hospitality. There is *The New Gold Standard* by Joseph Michelli, which details the success of the Ritz-Carlton Hotel Company. There's *Be Our Guest*, written by the Disney Institute, which explains the value of exceeding—rather than meeting— expectations. There's *The Disney Way* by Bill Capodagli and Lynn Jackson and *The Milkshake Moment* by Steven Little, recommended to me by Dr. Mike Ursu and Ken Varner, Global Director of Professional Relations and Dental Education at Zimmer Biomet. I must admit, I haven't read them thoroughly. But I know that none of them addresses hospitality in the medical office. Though Danny has long been an inspiration, for the most part, I didn't design our office's philosophy of culture and service by reading books.

I've developed our approach by being a good observer— seeing what works and what doesn't. One of my close friends and co-teachers on human relations, neuro-linguistic programing (NLP), and customer service, John O'Connor, calls me unconsciously competent. I have learned most of what I do in my practice by watching and experiencing how other successful businesses, particularly those in the hospitality sector, make people feel. John has been very instrumental in making me aware of what I do intuitively. He is a brilliant teacher and has the ability to help his students and clients navigate what he calls the banks of the river.

That brings me to another powerhouse name in dining that has had a tremendous impact on me, one you're probably familiar with: Zagat. Husband and wife Tim and Nina Zagat were practicing attorneys who met at Yale Law School in the 1960s. More than anything, they loved going out to eat. They founded the Zagat Survey in 1979 to crowdsource and share diners' opinions on local restaurants. The first Zagat Survey covered New York City and included one hundred reviews from their friends. Later, the company expanded to encompass seventy cities and thousands upon thousands of reviews from the public, rating not just restaurants but hotels, music venues, theaters, airlines, golf courses, and more.

ZAGAT®

The rating system was simple: guests evaluated restaurants based on three primary components: food, décor, and service. Each component received a rating, which constituted the total score. For fifteen years, Zagat named Danny Meyer's Union Square Cafe as New York's most popular restaurant in its annual survey. Why? Its food, décor, and service were exceptional. Each component contributed significantly to the customer-centric experience for which Danny Meyer is known.

That differs from what most would assume. If you were to ask the average foodie about the secret to most restaurants' success, they would probably say it's the food. That is certainly true some of the time. For example, Peter Luger has been a New York City institution for 133 years. It doesn't take credit cards—with the exception of its own. Guests usually have to wait for a table after they arrive, regardless of whether they have a reservation. The service is notoriously terrible. When you go to Peter Luger, you don't feel Danny Meyer's key tenet of hospitality: that the staff is on your side. The staff's surly nature has even become an element of the experience. Some say that this is part of the charm of the restaurant. They can get away with it because the steaks are great. Peter Luger may continue to be profitable, but for many other restaurants—and even more so in other industries—that simply isn't enough.

In *Setting the Table*, Danny Meyer explains, "You may think, as I once did, that I'm primarily in the business of serving good food. Actually, though, food is secondary to something that matters even more. In the end, what's most meaningful is creating positive, uplifting outcomes for human experiences and human relationships. Business, like life, is all about how you make people feel. It's that simple, and it's that hard[8]."

Whether you are selling oysters or hot dogs, knee replacements or dental implants, that remains the crux of Danny's message—and mine. It's all about hospitality and human connection, especially when your organization has something to do with the human body.

Any business follows a standard set of procedures. In a restaurant, customers order food from waiters who provide those orders to the kitchen staff who prepare the food—putting it on the grill, heating it to a certain temperature, plating it, placing it on the counter for delivery to the dining room, and so on. In a dental or medical office, when someone comes in with a particular complaint, we follow a specific course of action too. Those processes require training, just as they do in a kitchen (we'll discuss this when we talk about treatment planning).

To become a periodontist, I completed college, dental school, a hospital-based general practice residency, and a residency in periodontics. I've taken multiple courses throughout the United States and around the world on different techniques, studying with practitioners who are leaders in their fields—from courses on implantology at the Brånemark Clinic in Gothenburg, Sweden, to lessons on the phenomenon of bone regeneration with Dr. Istvan Urban in Budapest, Hungary, and Drs. Craig Misch and Mike Pikos in Florida, sessions with master surgeons Markus Hurzeler and Otto Zuhr in Munich, Germany, as well as hours spending time with Maurice Salama, David Garber, and Christian Coachman both in Atlanta and in Brazil. The receptionists and hygienists in my office have gone through their own training as well.

Answering a phone, filing a chart, conducting a cleaning, fixing a broken tooth, placing an implant—the "whats" and "hows" of dentistry—are quite mechanical. People don't really care about the whats and the hows. They don't want to know exactly how their food gets to the table or what it takes to fill a cavity. Contrary to popular belief, they're not paying for those processes either; instead, they're buying a business's *why*.

What's Your Why?

Author and speaker Simon Sinek talks about the power of finding one's *why*, which he defines as "the purpose, cause, or belief that drives every one of us[9]." In his TED Talk on the subject, he explains that being able to articulate one's *why* fuels transformative leadership—that the passion and purpose inherent in the *why* naturally attract others. My *why* is the human connection that is fundamental to hospitality. **I am dedicated to cultivating that connection with every patient who walks through my doors.**

My *why* is the human connection that is fundamental to hospitality.

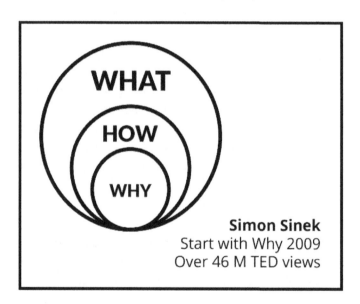

Simon Sinek
Start with Why 2009
Over 46 M TED views

My practice's mission statement is "to improve the quality of our patients' lives through education and motivation in a comfortable, caring, and friendly environment." My team and I developed this mission statement more than three decades ago, and it remains unchanged. It sums up our purpose, our *why*. The way we deliver the dentistry our patients need—from the moment they walk into my office until their course of treatment is complete—reflects our commitment to this mission statement. That's what sets my practice apart. The way you do what you do—whether you're serving sandwiches, baking a soufflé, taking blood pressure, or whitening teeth—reflects your *why*. If you directly connect your mission to the human beings purchasing from or interacting with you, you have a much higher chance of being successful than if you don't. Why? What we all want and need, more than anything else, is human connection.

We often think that meeting the needs of others has to do with our technical expertise—with a perfectly cooked filet, flawless color matching, a surgery that leaves no scarring whatsoever. Most of the time, though, that's just not the case. I've met plenty of patients who profess their love for their doctor (and remain loyal to that doctor) despite receiving mediocre care. They travel two or three hours to see someone who is essentially incompetent. And they often tell me all this when they come to see me to correct that individual's mistakes.

Every day, people visit diners and dive bars and neighborhood bistros not because the food is extraordinary, but because they want to go "where everybody knows [their] name." Now, I'm not saying subpar food, medicine, or dentistry is the norm; **I'm trying to show you how powerful hospitality is when it comes to the experience you provide.** Just as in the restaurant business, in medicine and dentistry the true trifecta—the true win—occurs when you can achieve high scores in each of Zagat's primary categories: clinical results (food), décor, and service.

Most dentists and physicians, however, don't consider and give equal weight to each of these components; most of us are born technicians. The field interested us because we like to do stuff with our hands—to take things apart and put them back together. We like operating. We like drilling holes and filling them. **We are proceduralists, not only because it is in our nature but also because it is what we learned in school. When we get caught up in procedures, it's easy to forget about the human beings who need our help.** There have been times when I have been working on a tooth only to look down and realize there is a human being attached to it, and I know I'm not alone.

But our patients are not procedures—that heart attack in Room 314 or the root canal or dental implant in Room 5—they are people. It's our responsibility to treat them with respect and kindness. If the patient doesn't feel good about the experience, they're not going to heal as well. Furthermore, scores of studies have shown the impact of stress on the body, spurring everything from periodontal disease to psoriasis to heart disease. By the same token, as medical professionals, we can help reduce stress and its effects simply by making people feel loved and cared for. We don't do that when we see them as procedures.

It's up to us to counter our nature, our education, and the way we've been socialized within our respective professions to provide the kind of care our patients deserve. We must take it upon ourselves to embed the tenets of hospitality into our approach and our practices. I'm not saying it's easy—there's a reason I'm writing this book now rather than at the beginning of my career. It took a lot of experience for me to develop my understanding of hospitality, and experience takes time.

Meanwhile, technology continues to advance at a breakneck pace. Today, patients have more information and options than ever in the form of online reviews, telehealth, state-of-the-art tools, and more. As a result, people will expect more from you and your practice, not less. You'll have to provide more than just good food.

More than Just Good Food

Here's an example. My daughter Becky was attending dental school at the University of Texas, in San Antonio. One day, she called me to ask whether I knew of any dermatologists in the area. I reached out to my dermatologist, Professor Jean Bolognia, at Yale University School of Medicine. She is one of the leading experts on malignant melanoma in the world and a coauthor of *Dermatology*, the dermatology textbook used in every residency program in the country. In short, she is the real deal. Dr. Bolognia gave me the name of a San Antonio dermatologist known to be among the best in the field, and I shared it with my daughter.

A few weeks later, I called to check in. "Did you see the doctor?" I asked her.

"No," she said, "I saw someone else."

"Why?"

"Have you seen his Google reviews?" I hadn't. "He only has three stars," she told me. Now, those reviews don't reflect his skills as a doctor. What they may represent is the way he runs his office, how his staff treats patients, or the manner in which those at the front desk answer the phone. Still, those reviews made an impact on my daughter, and she chose to see someone else. It turns out that she is in the majority. An NRC Market Insights study found that over 60 percent of patients chose a physician based on positive online reviews and that slightly more avoided one because of negative ones.[10] Chances are, that number is only going to grow.

Hospitality—your ability to make patients feel comfortable, cared for, and confident in their treatment—can fuel others' positive perception of your office and land you new patients that might otherwise never have called you. What does that look like in a dental or medical office? To understand, let's first consider the restaurant world.

In my favorite restaurants, the environment is not pretentious. I understand all the words on the menu. The waiters don't arrive at my table dressed in tuxedos or rattle off the specials in French. They are always kind and down-to-earth. When I ask a question, they don't use it as an opportunity to show off. They never make me feel inferior for not knowing the difference between semifreddo and sorbet. Instead, they help me weigh my interests and current circumstances—which may be as simple as whether I'm in the mood for fish or poultry—to make a decision I'll be happy with.

In my office, my team and I work to provide a similar experience. Patients receive personalized attention from the moment they walk in, from the wide variety of magazines available to them to the fact that they never have to wait more than five minutes before a staff member takes them to a treatment room. When I come in to see them, I introduce myself as Dr. Mike Sonick, and I invite them to call me Mike. I take time explaining everything. I provide them with options. I may tell new patients my story, which we covered in Chapter 2, but I also ask about theirs. *Where are you from? Are you new in town?* And most important, ***How can I help you?***

If a mother has driven two hours for her son's appointment—a procedure that will take hours on top of that—I'll ask about how she plans to fill that time and offer suggestions.

"Do you like baked goods?" I might ask.

If she responds that she's a foodie, I'll tell her that the best French bakery I've ever been to, Isabelle et Vincent, is four hundred yards from my front door. Before I've even finished my sentence, my assistant will already be printing out directions with the name and phone number of the bakery and jotting down her suggestions.

"You know," my assistant will add, "The cheese shop, Fairfield Cheese Company, across the street is great too!"

We have a five-page handout of the best places to eat, relax, and explore in the area. We give it to every new patient because many of them are new to town or just don't know as much about the area as I've learned by having lived here for forty years. One of the lists we provide is called "Fairfield Hidden Gems." It highlights the best places to hike, bike, and swim in Fairfield. As soon as I mention a local spot, whether it's a restaurant or outdoor trail, my staff has the information we have compiled ready. **It's part of our commitment to give everyone a "wow" experience—something extra they weren't expecting.**

That's also why I ensure that my team calls patients shortly after a procedure, and I follow up personally twenty-four hours later. It's why I might give someone six toothbrushes for their family, a bottle of prescription mouthwash, or a small package of antibiotics so they don't have to wait in line at the pharmacy to pick it up. These small gestures don't cost me much, but they make a tremendous difference. **They provide patients with a priceless gift: time. If I can give patients the gift of time by making life a little easier for them, that's a big deal.**

By the same token, I recommend dentists and doctors not just in Connecticut but also across the country. If a patient is moving to Florida and needs a good periodontist for follow-up care or her daughter is looking for an ENT in Minnesota, I provide referrals. We have gone to great lengths to create a list of top doctors, not only in my specialty but in every medical field. My team and I listen closely to the experiences our patients have had with other health-care providers. When they are favorable, we ask for more detail and research the provider ourselves. Once satisfied that they live up to the "top doctors" designation, we add them to our list. We have found that it is not that difficult to find excellence in all fields in all parts of the world. All we have to do is ask.

Once, I got a call from a patient on a Sunday morning. She was in Paris, France, had a terrible toothache, and wondered whether I could help. Within a few minutes, I had reached out to a French colleague of mine, Dr. Anne Benhamou, who agreed to open up her office to take care of that patient on the spot-on Sunday morning!

When I make a referral, a member of my team always calls to book the appointment for the patient. In every circumstance, we remove any barriers to care that we can imagine. Why? We don't want to employ a Sales Prevention Team (more on that later). Our goal is to do the opposite: to show everyone we serve real hospitality—to ensure they know we are on their side. The result is what we call a "wow" experience that goes well beyond good dentistry. **We want to make sure that every patient has a "wow" experience each time they visit with us—from directions to a local restaurant to a referral and an appointment with an excellent cardiologist.**

As my friend Todd Williams says, we attempt to deliver the unexpected. It's human connection in its purest form.

The result is what we call a "wow" experience that goes well beyond good dentistry.

How do I know whether I'm hitting the mark and creating the kind of hospitality for which Danny Meyer has become famous? I return to those three primary components laid out by Tim and Nina Zagat: food (dentistry), décor, and service. In the chapters to come, we'll explore each of those components, beginning with the one responsible for the all-important first impression: décor.

Summary: Making Hospitality an Inherent Part of Your Practice

The true greats in any consumer-facing industry—like Bobby Stuckey and Danny Meyer—understand the value of hospitality for hospitality's sake. They don't do it for the money; they do it because they truly care. The excellent experience they provide as a result has fueled their success. How do you tap into your ability to provide an exceptional experience? As Simon Sinek instructs, you've got to find your *why*. Patients and diners alike don't care about the hows or whats. So take the time to develop an understanding of why you do what you do. Ultimately, that will come through to those you serve in the form of extraordinary service.

In addition, your hospitality goes a long way in terms of healing. When you provide a great experience, you automatically reduce stress and therefore do your part in alleviating the many ailments associated with it. To make sure our patients feel cared for, we must counter our technical nature and take the time to slow down and treat them as people— the way we would want someone to care for our loved ones. It won't necessarily be easy, but it will definitely be meaningful.

And in this day and age, with so many channels for patients to voice their opinions, your soft skills—how you treat them from the moment they walk through the door for the first time to the end of your time together, whether it's minutes, hours, or months of recurring appointments—matter.

Ask yourself what you can to do make your patients more comfortable and give them a "wow" experience. What can you do to remove any barriers they may encounter? Is it making a list of resources in your area, offering the prescription medication they'll need after their appointment, making a reassuring phone call after a procedure, or setting up an appointment for them to see another specialist? **Once you identify what might matter most to them, make it part of your protocol.**

How to Make Hospitality a Matter of Course

- Hospitality is essential to your success, regardless of the type of service you provide.

- The first step in providing a truly exceptional experience is tapping into your *why*. When you know why you do what you do, you'll have better insight into what your patients want from their time with you as well.

- Next, think about any and all blockages to care, and consider how you and your team can remove them.

- Don't be afraid to offer insight that falls outside the realm of your practice. Telling your patients about the best restaurant in town, the tutor who helped your children master algebra, or the acupuncturist who finally relieved your years of back pain will improve their experience too—and may even support their healing.

- Look to provide a "wow" experience at every visit.

Questions to Consider

As you think about how to infuse hospitality into your practice, consider the following questions:

- Perform a Zagat-style survey for your office. Imagine you're a patient. How would you rate the services provided; the hospitality of the whole team, from the receptionist to the doctor; the décor? Be as honest as possible.
- What blockages to care exist in your practice?
- How could you remove them?
- What is your *why*?
- Does your office have a mission statement?
- If so, does your team know it?
- Do they live it?
- If not, would you be willing to write it?
- What do you consider to be a "wow" experience?
- Describe some "wow" experiences you've had previously.
- Describe "wow" experiences that you or your team have provided.
- Do you make sure that every patient has a "wow" experience every time? If not, how will you change your approach going forward?
- Does your entire team realize the importance of connecting with patients each visit?
- Are you comfortable allowing your customers (patients) into your "kitchen"?
- Do you allow your patients to see your backstage?

4

White Sneakers

Crafting an Impeccable Office Environment

W hy is décor a crucial component of the hospitality trifecta? Our surroundings have a significant impact on
the way we feel, and that's especially true in medical
and dental offices—places where we are vulnerable.

Your décor sets the tone for anyone who walks in. It can
put them at ease—or do just the opposite. That concept
extends beyond furniture and throw pillows to every aspect
of your operation, from your clothing to your landscaping—
anything that makes a first impression. And one cannot
overestimate the power of first impressions, especially when
they have to do with health.

The Importance of First Impressions

About thirty years ago, I went to a doctor's office for a medical consultation. When I pulled up to his office, I already knew I didn't like the facility. Why? It was yellow.

Yellow is not a healing color. Rather than the calming energy of teal or the soothing essence of purple, yellow suggests jaundice. Worse, the building faced away from the midday sun, which only contributed to its pallor. Its alignment, or lack thereof, also violated a key tenet of feng shui—the Chinese practice of creating balance between the spaces we occupy and the natural world—adding to my unease.

When I walked through the office doors, something about the energy of the place just didn't feel right. When you step into a beautiful hotel, restaurant, museum, or physician's office, you are immediately put at ease. You're able to exhale.

Every home and office I've occupied has been sun-drenched. The vibe on entering just feels right. Not this place. It was as dark and dreary as I had imagined it would be from the parking lot.

In his book *Blink: The Power of Thinking Without Thinking*,[11] Malcolm Gladwell explains that we form impressions within just two seconds. Of course, that doesn't mean your first impression is accurate. You may meet someone who has just lost their job, or broken up with a partner, or returned from the hospital where their son was admitted because he fell off his bike and broke his front teeth. Circumstances can cause people to deviate from their true nature, giving you an inaccurate and perhaps unfavorable impression.

In *The 7 Habits of Highly Effective People*,[12] Stephen Covey recounts a particular Sunday morning subway ride. The car was quiet when a man and his children boarded the train. The man sat down next to Covey and closed his eyes, seeming to tune out everything around him. Meanwhile, the children were loud and rambunctious. They threw things and even pulled at the newspapers of the people on the train.

Covey was getting more annoyed by the minute. From the eye rolls and sighs around him, he could tell other passengers felt the same way. Finally, he asked the man to do something about it.

"Oh, you're right. I guess I should do something about it. We just came from the hospital where their mother died about an hour ago. I don't know what to think, and I guess they don't know how to handle it either."

Covey's belief that the man was just a bad parent dissipated as quickly as it had formed. Guilt and compassion replaced his frustration when the man shared his circumstances.

Unfortunately, we rarely get the opportunity to address those first impressions. You never know why someone else is presenting the way they are, but in those first two seconds, it doesn't matter; the impression forms instantly based on what you see or hear. When it came to that doctor's office, my first impression was decidedly unfavorable.

Construction Ahead

Before I tell you about the rest of the visit, though, let me tell you about my own office. When I bought my current building, I thought I was getting a good deal. In 2003, I paid over $1 million—a lot of money—but I figured that, since it was already a dental office, it wouldn't take much to transform it into the kind of practice I'd always wanted. I'd be saving myself some cash in the long run.

Turns out, I was very wrong. The office had two entryways, one in the front of the building and one in the back.

That prevented a smooth flow of traffic through the facility. The fact that all of the treatment rooms were clustered in the middle of the building only reinforced the chaotic pattern.

Ultimately, I had to redesign it from scratch. Contractors gutted it, taking each of the four floors down to the studs. The whole project took over a year and filled thirteen thirty-yard dumpsters along the way.

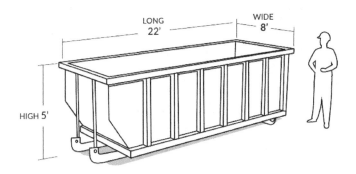

You'll remember that my dad was a carpenter. While I didn't inherit his construction skills, I did get his ability to design, plan, and envision a space. I have always been able to identify the details that go into creating an ideal outcome. When the remodel was complete, my building was beautiful inside and out. Having only one way to enter and exit eliminated the chaos and congestion. It was the kind of space I had been envisioning all along.

With the power of colors in mind, I painted the building a light taupe with pink undertones. Taupe is sophisticated, classic, timeless. I knew I couldn't go wrong with it. For the door, I chose a deep purple. I picked it because it's calming, but also because it's different. Purple is known for sparking creativity. Those who favor purple tend to be sensitive and compassionate, putting others before themselves. When it came to my practice, that was exactly the kind of message I wanted to convey to my patients: **In my practice, the patient comes first.**

One day, a patient of mine whom we'll call Donnie came in for a hygiene appointment. He was in the construction business and quite the character. His hair was big and coiffed. He favored tight T-shirts that strained against his chest, and a gold chain swayed around his neck at all times. He drove a Porsche—the fruit of his very successful labor as a developer. He was a larger-than-life type of dude and openly spoke his mind. I liked him.

"Mike," he said, "I really like what you've done with the building." My heart swelled with pride. The renovation cost had exceeded the purchase price by more than half. But in that moment, it all seemed worth it.

"But," he continued, "it just doesn't have any curb appeal." With that, I felt myself deflate.

He was right. I hadn't put anything into the exterior, in part because I had just lost my landscaper, Joe Palmieri.

Joe and I had been very close. We shared the same birthday—Earth Day, April 22—and had spent a lot of time talking about life and business over the years. Joe always had my back. About three weeks before I got married, I was in St. Petersburg, Russia, to give a lecture. Carole, my soon-to-be wife, and I were planning to get married in our backyard, and she called to tell me she was putting in some new steps in front of our house. Joe was doing the work.

"What kind of steps?" I asked. I didn't have much money at the time, and I had put what I did have into my practice.

"Oh, they're beautiful," she replied. "All slate and stone."

My mind began churning—I knew those steps had to be expensive—about $15,000, by my estimation. At that point in my career, I didn't have $15,000 for some steps. I was a little concerned about the cost.

When I got home, the project was complete. I took a deep breath, readying myself for a discussion about the cost, which we could not afford. But before I could say anything, Carole told me they were a wedding gift from Joe. That's just the kind of guy he was.

That winter, he passed. He suffered a major heart attack while he was plowing snow. He was only in his fifties. The loss hit me hard.

So Donnie was right—my building didn't have much curb appeal, because I didn't have anyone to tend to it. I was in the process of looking for another landscaper. Over the next year, I hired four landscapers—none of whom made the building look nice.

That is, until I found Andrew Kuczo. We met because he needed dental work done after a fight—one that had broken out in a country club, of all places.

Now, Andrew is one of the nicest guys I know. He's pretty soft-spoken. He's strong—he played lacrosse in college—but at around five feet nine, he's certainly not a big guy. You wouldn't peg him as the fighting type. And he wasn't.

But one evening, he was at the club with his wife and three daughters. A couple of men were drinking nearby. They began getting belligerent and loud. Andrew approached them in his mild-mannered way. He explained that his wife and daughters were nearby and asked whether they could keep it down.

That didn't sit well with one of the guys—all six feet four and 230 pounds of him. Without hesitation, he punched

Andrew directly in the mouth, knocking out his front three teeth and putting him in the hospital.

We met about a month later when I began rehabilitating his mouth—a process that would take more than a year. With all the time he spent in my chair, we got to know each other pretty well. I learned that he was a successful landscaper, though I wasn't familiar with any of his work.

When the rehabilitation was complete, I said, "You're a landscaper, right?"

"I am."

"Are you any good?" I asked.

"Yeah," he said, "I'm pretty good." He was modest but confident.

Having been through many contractors by that point, I had learned that it's a good idea to see someone's work before you hire them, so I asked for some of the addresses of the homes he had landscaped. "Sure," he said, and made me a list.

That weekend, Carole and I drove to each of the addresses he had jotted down. These weren't your average suburban homes; they were estates—each more beautifully landscaped than the next.

My lawn was quite small in comparison. *How can I ask him to work on my property when the rest of his clients have mansions?* I wondered. Still, I knew Andrew could provide the kind of curb appeal I desperately needed.

The following week, I gave him a call. "I saw your other properties," I told him. "Would you do my office?"

"For you, yes," he responded. "But only because you reconstructed my mouth."

"Do you do other places that small?" I asked him.

"No," he said.

After Andrew agreed to work with me, I took him to see some of the landscaping I liked. The nicest place I showed him was actually the Abraham Green Funeral Home—the only Jewish funeral home in Fairfield. Most funeral homes have beautiful landscaping. The owners know people are coming for a sad event. The last thing they want is to have them walk up to a building that makes them feel sadder.

"I can't make your building look like that," Andrew said.

"Why not?" I asked.

"You don't have any irrigation. If you want your property to look like that, we have to irrigate."

Within a few weeks, Andrew had pulled up the lawn and put in an irrigation system. Then he lined the entranceway with about twenty-five knockout rose bushes, which begin blooming in May and don't stop until Christmas. He placed two big pots alongside the building's entrance and filled them with seasonal flowers.

Andrew's six-man crew stops by every Tuesday. As soon as they arrive, my team begins timing them. It takes them about eight minutes to manicure my entire property to perfection: cutting the grass, raking the leaves, mulching—everything.

Sometimes on Sundays, Andrew comes by himself to plant flowers in those beautiful pots that flank the entrance.

What It Takes to Be Truly Exceptional

How many owners of successful companies work on the weekends, taking the time to go to their smallest client's office to do menial labor? Not many. Those who do are among the top 5 percent: those who are truly exceptional. Not everyone is good at what they do. Few are great. Even fewer are exceptional. Andrew is exceptional.

He owns the company with his brother and employs dozens of people, but he takes the time to do the little things that matter himself. It's a trait all of the greats have in common: they never forget what made them great in the first place. For Andrew, it is impeccable attention to detail and over-the-top customer service. His crew takes care of some of the largest estates on the Long Island Sound waterfront and the mansions that dot Fairfield County, yet on weekends, he is planting flowers in my office atrium. Like Bobby Stuckey in his kitchen at Frasca, he knows that the little things are important, and he's there to make sure they're done right. (See The Little Things in the Appendix for tips and ideas on where to make improvements in your place of business.)

Not a day goes by when two or three people don't say to me, "I love what you've done with the landscaping." It makes a powerful first impression. It's something I didn't really think about, even when I spent more on the renovation than I'd paid for the building, but I cannot overstate its impact. And not a day goes by when I don't think of Andrew and his exceptional work. The greats do it because they have no choice—it is in their DNA.

Of course, we're not all born with the ability to jump four feet in the air and dunk a basketball, play Beethoven's fifth by ear, or paint like Michelangelo, but everyone has the ability to be the best they can be. Everyone has a unique quality or skill that has the potential to make them great, what my mentor Dan Sullivan calls one's Unique Ability. If you happen to do that for a living, you're on your way to crafting an extraordinary life. To be compensated for something you would do for nothing is the greatest possible joy. But being great is also a choice. You may have the skills or the training, but it's something you decide to do day after day.

Three Specks of Blood

With that in mind, let's go back to that drab yellow doctor's office. I had gotten a bad vibe before I even stepped through the office doors—before interacting with a single human being. I didn't like that yellow building or that it sat angled away from the sun. Those factors shaped an impression in my mind of the doctor before our first meeting.

When it was time for the consultation, the doctor sat down across from me. He was nice enough. He sounded like he knew what he was doing. But as he was talking, I looked down at his sneakers. They were white, except for what looked to me like three specks of blood.

Right then, I thought back to my first trip to India in the early 1990s, before the internet and globalization became what they are today. Dr. Kumarswamy and Dr. Ajay Kakar had invited me to lecture to the Indian Academy of Periodontology at the first International Society of Aesthetic Plastic Surgeons Symposium in Mumbai (then Bombay), teach local dentists, and perform some periodontal surgery at Bombay Hospital.

I traveled with my close friend and fellow periodontist Dr. Robert Faiella, who would go on to become the esteemed president of the American Dental Association as well as one of the directors of the American Board of Periodontology.

We met when we were both taking our first implant course at the Brånemark Clinic in Gothenburg, Sweden. This was our first trip to India. We spent fourteen days teaching and traveling throughout the countryside. Being inducted into the Indian Academy of Periodontology added to this life-changing experience. I was the fourth non-Indian dentist to be inducted into the organization and was proud to be seated alongside the renowned Dr. Tomas Albrektsson from Gothenburg, Sweden, who along with P. I. Brånemark was a pioneer in implant dentistry and had been my first teacher of implant dentistry.

Back then, the hospitals in India didn't have a consistent sterilization protocol. Nurses readied the operating rooms by placing surgical tools on the same soiled drapes that had covered patients during the previous procedure. The doctors and nurses would walk from room to room with bare feet, flecked with blood from various patients.

Looking at those sneakers in that doctor's office in suburban Connecticut, those feelings I had in Bombay Hospital crept in. I knew then that the doctor didn't pay attention to details—and that just didn't bode well. As my good friend Dr. Istvan Urban of Hungary says, "The devil is in the details." He is known as the best in the world in vertical bone regeneration. In fact, he wrote the chapter on vertical bone growth in our original textbook, *Implant Site Development*.[13] Dentists from around the globe, myself included, fly to his private clinic in Budapest to study his masterful work, which few others are able to replicate. He pays attention to everything.

Back in the car after my consultation with the doctor, all I could think about were those blood-flecked sneakers. I never went back.

Were the yellow building or the blood on the doctor's sneakers true indicators of the quality of his work? I have no idea. What I do know is he made a strong first impression on me, and that was all that mattered. In my practice, I take great pains to ensure that every patient receives exceptional care and that we make the kind of positive first impression that leads them to trust us for that care. In addition to our beautiful building and its immaculate landscaping, I make sure to coordinate my team's appearance. Everyone wears the same uniform: jade scrubs—a color that has been associated with vibrancy and good health since the Victorian age. I make sure every employee has enough sets for the whole week so they don't need to wash them every day. In my own closet at home, I have twenty identical pairs.

Streamline to Address the Details that Matter

The average person makes thirty-five thousand decisions every day,[14] from what to eat for breakfast to what shirt to wear and which doors to go through. With so many choices in the world, not having to pick out what you are going to wear each day frees up some space in your brain for the decisions that matter. It's a good habit.

Albert Einstein bought several versions of the same gray suit because he didn't want to waste brainpower on choosing an outfit each morning. Now—decades later—former President Obama does the same, having limited his options to a gray or navy blue suit when the occasion calls for it. Steve Jobs became famous for the uniform of his choosing: a black turtleneck, jeans, and New Balance sneakers. One less decision allows one to focus on the important things—unless, that is, you are a Kardashian, making your living on social media. And if you like the one outfit you wear, you will feel good about your appearance.

I invest in another item for every member of my team. Can you guess what it is? That's right, white sneakers. They leave the sneakers in the office at the end of the day so they won't get dirty, and I buy them a new pair whenever the old ones need replacing.

I even put potential hires through a unique test. When someone comes in for a job interview, I ask them to bring a pair of white sneakers. If they forget or bring a less-than-perfect pair, it doesn't mean I won't hire them. But if they show up with brilliantly white sneakers, I know right away that they get it.

I always practice what I preach. I've been wearing clean white sneakers since I started my practice. I did it before I met that doctor in the yellow office because I thought it made a nice impression. And there was one day when I'd learn just how true that was.

A Lesson, Courtesy of Mario Sacco

I opened my first practice—an 850-square-foot office with two dental chairs—thanks to a $200,000 bank loan in 1985. Without much cash, I was the general contractor, architect, interior designer, and occasionally the plumber and house-keeper too. When I opened my doors, I had no patients and no referrals. To make things even more difficult, there were already five other periodontists in town—more than enough for a community of just sixty-five thousand. It was a crowded market. Everyone I met told me I had made a mistake by opening there.

But I figured that if five other guys were making a living, I could do it too. I wanted to be sure that was the case, so I solicited the advice of Dr. Michael Montanaro, my mom's orthodontist and a very successful real estate entrepreneur. Like the other greats I've encountered, he generously offered to meet with me. He brought me into his office, sat me down, and listened to my concerns. Then he gave me his advice: "If you want to build a successful practice, just do it," he told me.

"Keep in mind, though," he added, "you won't make any money your first year." To make up for the shortfall in my new practice, he instructed me to get a few jobs out of state. "That way," he told me, "The people in your community will only know you for your practice, not your job at the mall." I did just as he said. Today, people don't believe me when I tell them that I used to work in the Galleria Mall in White Plains, New York, and at the Holyoke Mall at Ingleside—outside of Springfield, Massachusetts.

Back then, I had an old stick-shift Volvo with 140,000 miles on it, and I'd rack up an extra 700 miles a week commuting between my apartment in Westport, Connecticut, to the Galleria Mall and to the Holyoke Mall, where I worked on weekends.

Dr. Montanaro was right about not making any money. My first year in practice, I grossed $35,000. My overhead was $90,000. Within fourteen months, though, I made enough money to quit my two mall jobs and focus on my own operation entirely.

About six years later, things were starting to come together. I had a healthy number of patients to my name, and one of them was Mario Sacco. Mario owned one of the most popular restaurants in the area—a real landmark, aptly named Mario's.

It was located right across the street from the Westport Train Station, and in between the 1960s and 1980s, commuters—*Mad Men*–type guys who traveled to and from

New York City for work—would step out of the train's bar car in the evenings and head straight to Mario's for their next drink. Artists and actors who lived in town would pile in too. Everyone loved Mario's, and my parents were no exception. They would go there almost every Sunday, a day when you couldn't get a seat unless you knew the *maître d'*.

It wasn't fancy—big round pine tables outfitted with captain's chairs packed the restaurant. Everyone said Mario's had the best martinis around. I don't know whether that's true. What I do know is that, for twenty years, Mario sold more liquor than any other restaurant in Connecticut.

Why? Mario was a great guy. He greeted everyone who walked through the door like family. He'd get to the restaurant around four-thirty or five and stay for about six hours, sipping his martinis, doling out hugs, and talking to people all night long. He always looked dignified—never sloppy—and he wore a beautiful jacket and tie. It was the experience—not the food—that had people coming back night after night for decades.

When he walked into my office, I felt as if I were treating my first movie star. His restaurant was the place to be. He seemed as connected as he was kind, and I figured that if I treated him well, he'd tell everyone he knew about me.

At that time, he was probably about eighty years old—and he needed a lot of dentistry. After the examination, I led Mario back to my office to discuss his case. Today, I stick to the same process; I examine the patient in a treatment room and speak with them in another—a dedicated consultation room. Back then, I brought patients to my private office, because I didn't have much space.

Mario and I sat at a round butcher block table, and I kicked off the conversation by telling Mario how much my parents—who had passed away by then—had loved his restaurant. After some reminiscing, I began to describe the treatment he needed. He didn't know a lot about dentistry, and he told me so. "I want to come back with my girl," he said. Mario had been married to the same woman for fifty years, and she had passed away the year before. When he came for the second visit, he brought a much younger woman with him—she was at least thirty years his junior. I immediately disliked her. The first thing I thought was that she was with him for his money. I figured she probably wouldn't want him to spend that cash on his teeth since there would be less for her to inherit when he died.

The stories I thought up about her ran through my head as I led them back to my office. In those days, I didn't have the training in neurolinguistic communication skills that I do now. I couldn't always connect with people, and it showed. I developed a whole host of assumptions about her.

Judging others serves to block positive human interactions. It creates distance rather than bringing people together. It also has the potential to inhibit your work. As dentist Dr. Milton Glicksman once wrote in *AAP News*, "Do not prejudge. Not every patient can afford all that we have to offer, but it's our responsibility to offer everyone the options that are available."[15] Today, I believe that everyone has the capacity for good, and I look for it in everyone I meet. But back then, I wasn't quite there. I engaged in what a lot of people do, false storytelling—telling ourselves a tale of our own design to explain a particular outcome and confirm our assumptions.

When we began talking, I bristled slightly—and so did she. In those first few moments, I could tell she didn't like me either. Malcolm Gladwell might say we both had negative blinks toward each other.

We made very little eye contact as I explained what Mario needed and what the options were. When I did look at her, she would look down at the floor. When I finished my monologue, Mario said, "I'll get back to you."

I didn't feel good about the visit. I was sure they wouldn't be back. Even then, I knew that when someone tells you they'll get back to you, chances are they won't.

Today, I know how to deal with patients' reservations during that first appointment. I always address any concerns before they leave because I know if they walk out that door with a promise to think about it rather than a follow-up appointment, I probably won't see them again.

Let's face it: no one wants to see the dentist. They don't want to make an appointment. When patients say they're going to think about it, they don't. It's a line. These days, when someone tells me they'll think about it, I say, "When are you going to think about it, next Tuesday?" I ask them if it's money, or fear, or a lack of information holding them back. I know it's my job to speak to every worry they may have. Why? I find that most people do not go home and think about it. There are so many things competing for their attention—significant others, children, work decisions, and yes, even what to wear—that they usually do not allocate a time to make those decisions, no matter how important.

It's important to note, too, that there are two primary blockages to care: apathy and fear. I can't do much about apathy. If someone does not care about their health and well-being, it is difficult to motivate them to take care of themselves. Fear is very different. Fear is an emotion aroused by a sense of impending pain or danger. It is an instinctual reaction, and we have instincts for a reason. It can be beneficial, protecting us from real risks. But fear isn't discerning. Threats—real and imaginary, rational or not—trigger fear.

In some cases, fear leads to panic, during which people are unable to think clearly or make good decisions.

Outsized worries about the unknown often keep people from seeing doctors—especially surgeons or dentists. **Those worries keep people paralyzed, avoiding the office visits necessary to diagnose or eliminate disease.** I have seen many of my friends and their parents suffer from illnesses—colon cancer, prostate cancer, hypertension, periodontal disease, and more—that could have been prevented or quickly treated with a simple test. Fear of the unknown often overshadows the real problem until that problem grows too big to be ignored. That's what I try to avoid during my consultations.

> **Outsized worries about the unknown often keep people from seeing doctors—especially surgeons or dentists.**

I attempt to educate patients, serving as a copilot or co-therapist so they can make informed decisions about their care. It's the first step in eliminating their fears—which we'll talk about in greater detail when we discuss treatment planning. But for now, let's talk about the kinds of fears that typically arise.

In my experience, those fears fall into three basic categories: pain, cleanliness (in the sense that they worry about getting an infection), and cost. Once I can identify the root cause of their fear, I can address it. A frank discussion can put the patient at ease.

Pain is the easiest to address, because local anesthesia and most over-the-counter pain medications mitigate any discomfort. I don't ask patients to take my word for it, though. Our website has more than one hundred videos in which patients discuss every aspect of their experience, from cost to discomfort and length of recovery. Over the years, we've found that seeing "normal" people just like them speaking about their experiences allays most patients' concerns. More than three thousand five-star patient reviews also help to alleviate worry.

Without me—or any professional—there to explain the procedure and direct them toward the resources available, however, they can't make a truly informed choice about their care. Asking patients *when* they plan to think about my treatment plan often startles them enough to generate further questions and conversation. The inquiry itself creates a willingness to discuss the decision-making process. When Mario was sitting in my office, however, I hadn't yet learned how to make all that happen.

What I did know is that I probably hadn't earned Mario's trust. Instead, I had assumed that his decision depended on his girlfriend. I had also assumed that she didn't like me—and I was too arrogant to put in the time to earn her trust too. Instead, I acted like a doctor. I told them what he needed, how I'd do it, how much it would cost, and what the success rate was. I didn't make them feel connected, loved, cared for, or safe. I didn't do my part to allay their fears.

When Mario came in two weeks later for a third appointment, I was surprised that he was alone. "Do you want to sit in the treatment room so I can look in your mouth?" I asked him.

"No," he said. "We've already done that. I just want to talk to you alone."

We went back to my private office, to the round butcher block table.

"I think I'm going to do the treatment," he said.

I was blown away. "Okay," I said.

"How much will it be?" he asked.

Now, I had already told him how much it would cost: $9,000—a lot of money to a young dentist like me.

"Okay, I'd like to pay you half now," he said.

In that moment, he made eye contact with me. I knew enough to know that Mario was smart. He was a good businessperson. He knew more about human relationships than I did. I figured he was looking at me to see if I was excited, to see if I cared more about the money than about caring for him.

"Is it okay if I pay you in advance?" he asked. He was an eighty-year-old man looking at a thirty-five-year-old kid—a kid he likely thought was in debt from all those years at school—to see whether I'd jump at that money. I wasn't going to take the bait.

"You can if you want to; it's entirely up to you," I replied.

"I'll give you half now," he repeated, pulling a checkbook from his pocket. He made out a check for $9,000.

"I thought you were going to pay me $4,500," I said.

"No," he responded, "I'm going to give you the whole thing." The treatment would take about six months. It wouldn't even begin for another month. Still, he had given me the money. It was a display of trust.

Meanwhile, I knew I had been prideful, arrogant, and even a little bit snippy as I told myself those stories about his girlfriend and their relationship. I wanted to know why he wrote me that check. So I asked.

"Mario," I said, "I'm surprised that you came back."

"Why?"

"I could tell your girlfriend didn't like me."

"Yeah," he said, "and you didn't like her either. But she was really impressed."

"By what?" I asked.

"Your white sneakers."

I looked down and there they were—as clean as the day I had bought them. I had known they were important, but I hadn't realized they were that important. Despite my prickly demeanor, my sneakers had managed to make a strong first impression.

Meanwhile, I learned that my impression of Mario's girlfriend had been off. Yes, she was younger than Mario, but she was also caring and smart—she had a doctorate in education. Eventually, she became my patient too. Above all, she taught me the true significance of a pair of white sneakers.

Your décor, your appearance, your efforts to go out of your way to impress your patients up front may seem trivial, but I assure you they are not. They speak volumes about who you are and what you can do. More than that, they make a difference in your patients' experience, and that's a priceless investment.

With that in mind, it's time to talk about service.

Summary: Crafting an Image That Reflects the Quality of Your Approach

Although the appearance of your building, grounds, and staff may seem trivial, these factors make the all-important first impression and set the tone for the patient experience. As such, décor is a vital consideration for any practitioner. One has only to think about their experiences as a patient walking into a new practice—or reflect on the one I share in this chapter—to understand the value of getting the optics right.

Of course, first impressions aren't always accurate. However, whether or not they are a true reflection of the quality of your practice matters little because patients often make decisions about whether to work with you based on what they can see from the outside.

It's not only the first impression that makes an impact; the details matter too. Those who are truly great take the time to do the little things. They don't do what they do for the money; they do it because it's in their DNA. More than that, they do it because they never forget how they got where they are today.

Everyone has the potential to be great—a unique talent or ability that sets them apart. Tapping into it and making sure it shines will allow you to do excellent work—and love what you do. Keep in mind, though, that you've got to commit to it too. Greatness is a choice—one we make every single day.

In my office, I do everything I can to ensure that we make a great first impression and that my patients receive the kind of care that echoes it, in which every detail is attended to. Everyone wears the same uniform in a soothing shade of jade, and they all have perfectly pristine white sneakers—an element that has long played a role in my success. The scrubs and sneakers not only send a message about the cleanliness of my office and the seamlessness of my approach—they also mean there is one less decision I have to make each day, freeing up my mind to focus on the important things.

Though you must account for the reality that patients will certainly judge you on your appearance—the sneakers and more—you must do your best to avoid judging them. Doing so will only block your ability to connect. Instead, offer each person the same experience, treatment options, and advice. Remember Dr. Milton Glickman's quote: "Do not prejudge. Not every patient can afford all that we have to offer, but it's our responsibility to offer everyone the options that are available."

It's also your job to address any concerns your patients may have. There are two primary blockages to care: apathy and fear, and while you can't do much about apathy, there are numerous ways to make them feel more comfortable about the situation at hand.

How to Make Sure You're Conveying the Right Message

- Your décor (which is, for our purposes, every visual aspect of your practice) sets the tone for the patient experience and can be a determining factor in whether patients choose you for their care. Thus, it must be a priority.

- If you want to build a successful practice, follow the advice of Dr. Michael Montanaro: Just do it.

- Don't judge your patients. Offer everyone the same experience, treatment options, and advice.

- Don't send them home to "think about it"; walk them through the options and help them come to the right decisions, assuaging their fears along the way.

- Educated patients make the best decisions.

Questions to Consider

As you evaluate your approach to your practice's décor, consider the following questions:

- How has the appearance of other medical or dental offices influenced your experience or decisions as a patient?

- Can décor make us feel less vulnerable—more comfortable?

- What décor decisions can you make to put your patient at ease?
- Is your team professionally and uniformly attired?
- Is there a uniform protocol in place?
- Can you institute changes that improve both the optics of your practice and your experience as a provider?
- Do you feel that fear is a major blockage to care?
- How do you address a patient who is fearful of care?
- What can you do about apathy?
- Do you feel cost is a major blockage to treatment?
- What strategies does your office use to remove cost as a barrier?
- What changes can you make immediately to improve the patient experience?
- Are you willing to make those changes? If not, why not?

5

A Tale of Health Care in Two Cities

Overcoming the Challenges of the American Health Care System

In the best hotels and restaurants in the world, the service customers receive—and the exchanges they have with the staff—matter a great deal. That's just as true in medicine and dentistry. As such, each interaction a patient experiences, from the moment they walk through your door to the day their treatment is complete, must be pleasant, seamless, and exceptional.

To highlight the value of such an experience, let me tell you about two very different medical processes I went through to address the same problem.

About six years ago, my wife and I were in Buenos Aires, Argentina, visiting our son, Jason, who was living there at the time. I had just finished one of the busiest months of my career—seeing more patients and doing more complex procedures than I would have imagined possible in previous years.

During our trip, we decided to go to Chile for the day, which was just a two-hour flight from Buenos Aires. When we arrived, we rented a car to explore the landscape. Well, I don't like to drive, and I'm not very good at it either, as many of my passengers will attest. But because I'm somewhat of a traditional male and because I was with my wife in a different country, I insisted on taking the wheel. She agreed—which was probably a mistake, as it was also a stick shift.

As you might expect, I found driving in Chile even more stressful than driving in Connecticut. My palms got sweaty. My blood pressure rose. And then I felt my vision start to go.

The Physical Toll of Stress

I had long known how powerful stress could be. Medical providers of all types are well aware that stress can—and does—lead to disease. In dentistry we see the effects that stress can have on the body. Under stress, patients grind their teeth (bruxism), leading to wear (attrition), TMJ disorders, and muscle soreness. Under stress, disease can progress rapidly and delay healing after surgery. Most dentists know that stress can lead to acute necrotizing ulcerating gingivitis (ANUG), a disease that results in the death of dental papillae (the pointy triangle of gum tissue that sits between the teeth). The papillae ulcerate and necrose, and patients can experience burning and severe pain as well as a bad, metallic taste in their mouths.

The harmful bacteria that lead to ANUG can increase under significant stress. You might know ANUG under a different name: trench mouth. Where did it get its moniker? During World War I, soldiers frequently developed gum problems caused by the stress that arose in the trenches and the lack of available dental care.

During the early 1980s, when I was a resident at Metropolitan Hospital, an inner-city hospital serving Spanish Harlem in Manhattan, patients with ANUG began flooding in. At first, I thought they were just stressed out. I would later learn it wasn't just frazzled nerves; it was AIDS—acquired immune deficiency syndrome, a new disease that we were just beginning to diagnose and discover.

When human immunodeficiency virus (HIV) transforms into full-blown AIDS, the relationship between T cells—lymphocytes that play a key role in the immune response—and B lymphocytes—white blood cells that produce antibodies—changes. HIV attacks the body's T cells, depleting them to such low levels that they cannot signal B cells to secrete antibodies. Without T and B cells working in tandem to prevent infection, the body can't fight off harmful bacteria as well as it could before.

Research shows that the stress students experience when studying for final exams has a similar effect on T and B cells. Stress alone led to the loss of gum tissue. When final exams ended—along with the corresponding stress—and students went on summer vacation, B and T cells resumed their healthy relationship. Doctors often tell patients that it's all in their head. There's a lot of truth to that. But thoughts and feelings have a significant impact on what's happening in the body, a reality that unfolded for me as I made my way down an unfamiliar Chilean road in that rental car.[16]

With a thorough understanding of stress's myriad effects on the body, I figured that the anxiety driving that day and the hectic months before it was to blame for my vision issues. I also figured that it was my body finally relaxing and letting go from the previous month of long hours performing dental surgery. So we flew back to Buenos Aires, and I tried to get some rest. When I woke up the next day, the room was spinning. I tried to focus, but I couldn't. To my left, I saw two of my wife, both asking in unison whether I was okay.

As a doctor, I knew double vision was not a good sign—particularly since I'd never had it before. A dear friend of mine had recently been diagnosed with brain cancer. He was dying. I was convinced that I either had a brain tumor myself or that I had just suffered a stroke.

"We need to find a hospital," I told my wife. I don't speak Spanish, and neither does she. My son, Jason, was new to the country, having just moved there a few months earlier, and although he's fluent today, back then he couldn't do much more than order a drink at a *restaurante* or get directions to *la playa*. That wasn't going to be very much help as we attempted to scout out a hospital in a non-English-speaking country. I was sure that I didn't have much time to live and could feel my anxiety level rising.

When we walked into the closest hospital, the person manning the front desk told me they didn't treat eye problems there and suggested I go to the nearby eye clinic.

At the eye clinic, I met a young girl who didn't speak a lick of English. I tried to tell her what was wrong anyway. She just kept repeating *doble, doble, doble*—meaning double in Spanish—and then gestured for me to take a seat.

Finally, she brought me back to meet the doctor, Dr. Mauricio Martinez Cartier. I did not know it at the time, but he was the director of the Institute of Vision. Thankfully, he spoke fluent English. After listening to my ordeal and examining me for a few minutes, he said, "I think I know what you have. It seems like avascular necrosis of the small artery that leads to the left lateral rectus of your eye. In most cases, vision returns to normal in about three months."

Throughout the examination, he was elegant and articulate—providing a quality of care no different from what you'd expect from a Harvard-trained ophthalmologist. He put me at ease with his kind, calm demeanor, and I was certainly relieved by the diagnosis itself. But I wanted to make sure we ruled everything out. "Great," I told him, "But we should get a CAT scan." He nodded and helped me make arrangements for the scan. Then he gave me his cell phone number and email in case I needed anything else.

The Cost of Care in the United States and Abroad

Because we were in Argentina, I had to pay out of pocket for the procedure on the spot. It cost me a whopping $15.

The next day, I got my CAT scan. The clinic wouldn't release the results to me, so I asked that they be sent to my new Argentinian doctor and paid out of pocket again for the scan—$100 in total.

The following day, I returned to the doctor's office. I didn't have an appointment; I just walked in. As I passed by the door to his office, I nodded at him, and he waved me in.

"Your scans look clear," Dr. Cartier said. "I was right—your vision will come back completely in three months."

"Okay," I said, not entirely convinced. "Is there a fee today?"

"No," he replied. I thanked him and went on my way.

The next day, I came by to check in with him again—I wanted to be sure everything was all right. Again, I passed by his office, he waved me in, and we talked. In the days that followed, I called twice more, just to follow up, and emailed one more time. It's hard not to seek reassurance after believing one's life is on the line—particularly in another country. Each time, he assured me I'd be fine.

Three visits, two calls, and one email with an exceptionally competent and professional physician. The total cost? $115—the $15 charge for my first visit and $100 for the CAT scan were all I paid.

When I got back to the United States, I was still nervous. It just seemed too easy. So, although my wife insisted I was fine, I scheduled an appointment with my regular ophthalmologist. "This is something we don't treat here," he told me once I'd submitted my co-pay and settled into the chair in his office. "You need a neuro-ophthalmologist."

I scheduled an appointment with a team of neuro-ophthalmologists at Yale. After around three hours of treatment, they suggested I have two magnetic resonance imaging (MRI) scans—one with contrast and one without. Then it was back to their office for more treatment and therapy. The bills for the MRIs and visits? About $15,000.

To cover all the bases, I added an Eastern complement to all this Western medicine, seeing an acupuncturist who put needles into my eye for six visits at about $300 per session. Neither effort—Eastern nor Western—had an effect on my vision.

Three months to the day after that ophthalmologist in Buenos Aires said my vision would return to normal, it did. I've never had a problem since. It turned out that that $15 visit and a $100 CAT scan were all I needed.

The doctors I saw in the United States were perfectly nice, though my visits certainly had a more clinical feel compared with my strolls through the Argentinian doctor's office. Each time I visited the Yale office, I had to stand in line to check in and then take a seat in a waiting room where multiple signs informed patients that they would need their insurance card before they could see a doctor.

"If you have a co-payment, it is due now," another set of signs stated. Each sign, posted on a glass window that separated me from the receptionist on the other side, served as a barrier to entry. There was no way I could have walked into one of my doctors' offices on a Thursday afternoon without an appointment.

How was my experience in the United States overall? In a word, expensive. Meanwhile, none of the tests or treatments did anything to ameliorate my condition. The only thing that worked was *time*, something the Argentinian doctor had suggested from my first visit.

With my vision returned and my neuro-ophthalmology experience concluded, I wrote to Mauricio Martinez Cartier, my Argentinian doctor. I let him know the experience he'd provided was one of the best I'd ever had in medicine, telling him that if there was ever anything I could do to return the favor, to please give me a call.

Mauricio wrote back. Today, I have a personal relationship with him. As I said, the other doctors I saw were nice. They were competent. But to them I was just another patient—a series of codes to submit to the insurance companies. Now that's not to say they ran those tests just to make money. They did it because that's what physicians are trained to do. They are trained to do procedures and must code them so that health care insurance will reimburse them for their time.

The Argentinian doctor took me into his office. He realized I was from another country, that I didn't speak the language, and he did something for me that went beyond diagnosis, testing, and treatment. He told me it was going to be okay and that he'd take care of things to ensure that was true. **He made a human connection with me. He gave me a "wow" experience.**

Sir William Osler said, "The good physician treats the disease; the great physician treats the patient who has the disease." That's what the Argentinian doctor did.

The History of American Health Insurance

So why were my experiences in Argentina and the United States so wildly different? Much of it comes down to health insurance.

Back in 1900, when doctors prescribed literal snake oil to treat a multitude of ailments, health care cost the average American about $5 per year—just $150 today when you factor in inflation. Health insurance wasn't necessary because health care was so inexpensive to begin with. But early in the twentieth century—with the development of antibiotics and other medicines backed by research (rather than old wives' tales) and formal medical training—hospitals transformed from dirty, dangerous places housing the poorest of the poor into clean, credible institutions with the potential to heal. The improvement in resources and care also cost significantly more money.

People weren't used to paying a lot of money for quality care. As such, they would visit a hospital only when death seemed likely—and pay a premium—but they weren't in the habit of getting regular checkups or coming in for less pressing illnesses.[17]

In the late 1920s, an administrator at Baylor University Hospital in Dallas, Texas, had an idea. What if people paid for medical care in installments over time? Doing so would seem less daunting than receiving a large medical bill and might encourage patients to seek treatment earlier and more often, which might help prevent serious disease. With that goal in mind, the institution launched its first health-care plan. Dallas public school teachers could pay fifty cents per month, and the hospital would cover the cost of their doctor's visits.

During the Great Depression, hospitals around the country adopted the strategy, which became known as Blue Cross.[18] Unfortunately, few people took advantage of the offering.

During World War II, when employers were desperately trying to meet the manufacturing demand, companies started offering fringe benefits as an additional draw, including health care. A series of associated tax advantages made it mainstream. By the 1960s, 70 percent of the population had private health insurance—primarily through their employers.[19]

Physicians were happy because they didn't have to worry about getting patients to foot the bill. To receive compensation for a particular procedure, either the physicians themselves or their billing departments would simply enter a code. More codes meant more compensation. Some physicians got good at stacking procedures. If you came in for chest pain, they'd do a full workup—ordering an echocardiogram and blood work, for example. **Soon, insurance became a double-edged sword. Health insurance covered those tests, but because of the creeping care costs, coverage was becoming more expensive too.**

In 1965, President Lyndon B. Johnson established a basic insurance program for citizens who didn't have health insurance, forming what would become Medicare and Medicaid.[20] However, corporate insurance companies and

Medicare and Medicaid alike had the same goal: to pay as little as possible.

With the advent of the DRG—or diagnosis-related group—in 1989, payment for various types of procedures became standardized with the goal of reining in inpatient hospital costs billed to Medicare.[21] Regardless of what a hospital spent to treat a particular patient, Medicare would pay a flat rate based on the diagnosis and corresponding DRG. That meant if you came in with pneumonia and stayed two days, accounting would assign you the same DRG as someone with the same diagnosis who stayed for ten days. Although the hospital might have made a bit of a profit on you, they would have undoubtedly lost money on the other guy.

Dentistry remuneration evolved very differently. In the United States, doctors and dentists belong to different groups with different sanctions, which isn't the case in every part of the world. In certain European countries, you have to go to medical school and then pursue dentistry as a specialty—just as you'd pursue psychiatry or emergency medicine. But the built-in difference in the United States led to a different approach to insurance for care.

The first dental insurance plans didn't emerge until 1954 when the Longshoremen's and Warehousemen's Union and the Pacific Maritime Association became the first group to request dental coverage as a fringe benefit, working with Washington, Oregon, and California dental societies to establish prepaid dental plans.[22]

In the 1970s, dental coverage became mainstream, offering patients approximately $1,000 toward their care annually. Today, decades later, most dental plans offer about the same amount of coverage—approximately $1,000 per year—as they did when the plans became mainstream in the 1970s. The only difference is that inflation has increased by about 567 percent. Thus, that $1,000 gets you very little dental work today. If dental insurance reimbursement kept up with inflation, then the average patient would receive close to $7,000 a year, not $1,000. Dental insurance today is not really insurance. It is a merely a small stipend.

Although medical and dental plans operate differently, health care at large has become big business, composing 17.1 percent of America's GDP.[23] Complications continue to grow as practitioners and medical facilities find new ways to bill—and insurance companies develop policies and practices to dodge those ever-increasing costs.

The legal profession only complicates those dynamics. In 2019, there were 6,350 dental school graduates, 26,641 medical school graduates, and 33,895 law school graduates.[24] With more law school graduates flooding the market, each year the competition for clients increases. More lawyers means more malpractice claims, and that means insurance costs for both physicians and dentists are going up. In turn, we have no choice but to raise the cost of our procedures.

Because medical professionals fear being sued for making an incorrect diagnosis, we conduct more tests so that no lawyer can tell us we missed something we should have caught. It's a perfect storm that results in the United States spending more on health care than any other country in the world—all while delivering poorer quality care than many of its wealthy peers. In a study of eleven countries, the United States had the highest health care earnings per capita but ranked last for health outcomes, equity, and quality.[25] Those factors along with the focus on numbers rather than service have essentially shattered the doctor–patient relationship.

It's a perfect storm that results in the United States spending more on health care than any other country in the world.

To avoid insurance complications, approximately 5 percent of dental practices today, including mine, are fee-for-service—they don't accept any insurance at all. When a patient comes in, I let them know what I see, what it will take to address the issues they have, and how much it will cost, and together we make a determination about what to do. It's a shared decision-making process. At that point, I present the patient with the fee. If patients have dental insurance, we submit the paperwork as a courtesy. They can accept it or not.

And because I don't answer to anyone except the patient with whom I partner in planning their care, I have the ability to decide whether I'm willing to do it for less money or complete just a part of the procedure. I can accept or decline their offer to trade me some chickens from their farm or haircuts at their salon for the work that needs to be done. We can negotiate.

That's not true in the traditional medical system, at least not for the most part. It's not unusual for patients to run up such high medical bills that, after insurance does its part, patients are left staring down a $100,000 tab they can't pay. When the hospital calls to collect, knowing there's a chance the institution may not get anything at all, there's sometimes room to negotiate. If you can pay the bill in three installments over the course of three months, the hospital may drop the fee by half. Fifty-thousand dollars, though, is a staggering amount that most people can't afford.

Despite the financial challenges and hurdles created by insurance companies, doctors still have a choice when it comes to the kind of service they provide. As someone fortunate enough to have good health insurance, the capacity to pay for quality care, and medical expertise myself, I have seen the upside and the downside of medical care in the United States.

Finding Quality Care in a Crowded Market

My daughter Becky was born with a big red hemangioma on her cheek. This was about thirty years ago, and my wife and I thought she would have to go through life with it. We took her to every physician we could find, including a pediatric dermatologist at Yale, Dr. Sidney Hurwitz, who had written a leading textbook on pediatric dermatology.

He greeted my wife, my daughter, and me in his office. He was wearing a white coat, the frayed collar of his oxford shirt peeking out from beneath it. He immediately pulled an old camera from his desk and began taking pictures of the hemangioma. He was visibly excited about this little patient and was brimming with compassion for all three of us. I knew from the research I had done that he was in his sixties—around the age I am now. He must have seen ten thousand or more hemangiomas by that point, and yet he made us feel as though her case was one of the most import-ant of his career. I felt safe and knew he had my daughter's best interest at heart. In fact, he told us he would not perform surgery on her. He informed us that conventional treatment might leave a scar. He recommended that we take Becky to Dr. Oon Tan, a leading dermatologist in Boston, who was a pioneer in nonsurgical laser therapy. We did, and after a few visits the hemangioma faded, miraculously.

A few years later, I needed a physician for a common procedure: a colonoscopy. My mother died of colon can-cer, which makes me more prone to the disease because of its heritability. My physician instructed me to schedule my first colonoscopy at age forty. Although I'm not anxious by nature, I worried about what the test might reveal. Denise, the wife of my closest high school friend, Pat Carroll, was a nurse in a gastroenterologist's office. She told me that although the doctor didn't have the best bedside manner, he was good at what he did. "Plus, I'll be there with you," she assured me.

My appointment was at nine in the morning on a Friday. I prepared for the test the day before, fasting for twelve hours and consuming only clear liquids. When I arrived at the hospital, a nurse instructed me to put on a gown—open at the back—and walk down the very public hallway to the room where the procedure would take place. I followed orders and shuffled down the hall, starving, dehydrated, and very nearly nude as I struggled to keep the gown closed. This was in pre-HIPAA days.

I settled myself on the table and waited for the doctor to arrive. "Where is the doctor?" I asked when the nurse came by to check on me.

"He's got an emergency," she said. "He'll be here soon."

One hour passed. Then two. Then three. The whole time, I sat on a cold gurney, making small talk with the nursing team.

The doctor finally arrived around twelve o'clock. He was visibly stressed, so much so that I felt that I should comfort him before he got to work. A colonoscopy is one of the more violating procedures one can have, and I certainly didn't want to feel the effects of his tension. He was very well dressed in a beautiful blue suit and a yellow tie, so I complimented his appearance, saying, "Well, you look elegant."

"It's an elegant procedure," he responded. "I know I'm late," he added, without apologizing. Rather than waiting for the anesthesiologist to arrive, the doctor began administering my anesthesia himself.

Halfway through the procedure, I woke up screaming. He hadn't given me enough medicine, and the tube he had inserted was pushing on a nerve plexus, causing me excruciating pain. I grabbed the sides of the gurney, screaming as loud as I could. "Please, please, pull it out!" I yelled. It took about ten seconds for the pain—the most excruciating of my life—to subside as the anesthesia kicked in again.

When I woke up again, I was in recovery. The nurse told me I could go. At least, I think that's what happened. Still groggy from the medicine and anxious about the tests potential outcome, I couldn't process a word she said. Soon, my wife, Carole, arrived. She took me to lunch, but I didn't feel like eating. I was too worried about the results.

On Saturday morning, I waited for a call from the doctor, the nurse, a hospital administrator—anyone—but my phone never rang. I had to do something to distract myself, so I decided I'd go buy a pair of sneakers—white, of course. I headed to an ATM to take out some money before going into the store, but I was so nervous that I forgot my pin number. *I'll just use a credit card*, I told myself.

In the store, I picked out four pairs, and the salesman went downstairs to see whether they had any in my size. *What are you buying sneakers for?* I thought. *You could have cancer. What are you going to do with new sneakers then?* Before the man could return with the shoes, I left the store, overcome with fear.

On Sunday, I called the office and left a message. No one called me back.

On Monday, three days after my colonoscopy, I called again. The receptionist eventually picked up and transferred me to the nurse. "Is everything okay?" I asked, breathless.

"You're fine," she responded.

All of a sudden, the anxiety lifted. Two words made all the difference. I only wish someone had made a fifteen-second phone call earlier to see how I was doing and give me the results.

All of our patients are provided with a phone number that will enable them to contact me or one of my practice partners twenty-four hours a day. I also make my personal email and cell phone available. In my practice, we call patients the night of surgery and the day after that. For the first twenty-four hours, patients typically aren't in any pain. A nurse makes the first call to assure patients that we are there for them. I call about twenty-four hours later to make sure they are doing well. I also provide simple advice on treating any pain or swelling, much of which is explained in the postoperative instructions we provide.

Checking in with my patients post procedure has been my protocol since I opened my practice. Just one post-procedure phone call would have saved me three days of pain, worry, and needless suffering after my colonoscopy. Much of that suffering was due to my emotions. We've already established the toll stress can take on the human body. For that reason, I share this story—and my practice's protocol—in many of the lectures I give. Calling patients is a small act of kindness and professionalism that can make a tremendous difference.

I'm part of Abundance360, a mastermind and executive program run by engineer, physician, and entrepreneur Peter Diamandis. One of the program's offerings includes a day at Health Nucleus, a leading-edge precision program that leverages premier technology to prevent and diagnose disease. The company takes a proactive approach to health care that aligns with my personal perspective, in which testing plays a key role in prevention and early intervention.

My evaluation at Health Nucleus included an MRI, whole genome sequencing with annual re-annotation, computed tomography (CT), echocardiogram, electrocardiogram (ECG), wireless heart rhythm monitoring, balance tracking, comprehensive laboratory tests and metabolic analysis, insulin sensitivity testing, DEXA (which measures bone mineral density and strength), and more.

When the results came in, I learned that, overall, my health was great. But I had a high coronary CT, or coronary calcium score, which is associated with calcifications of the coronary arteries. And since coronary artery disease runs in my family—my father died of heart disease at the age of eighty-four—and I personally had a history of high cholesterol, even in my early twenties, I knew I was prone to the disease myself.

Fortunately, Dr. Stuart Zarich—my colleague, friend, workout partner for the past twenty-five years, and Chief of Cardiology at Bridgeport Hospital—had recommended I go on a statin at the very beginning of our relationship, which had kept my cholesterol numbers low for more than two decades. Still, my CT score was a whopping seven hundred, indicating that I indeed had coronary artery disease.

I took that information to a team of doctors, including Drs. Bradley Bale and Amy Doneen who wrote the book *Beat the Heart Attack Gene: The Revolutionary Plan to Prevent Heart Disease, Stroke, and Diabetes*[26]. They believe that decreasing inflammation in the body through diet, exercise, and medication—if necessary—as well as preventing and treating periodontal disease can decrease the likelihood of coronary artery disease and stroke. As a matter of fact, Dr. Bale guarantees that if you have a heart attack or stroke under his care, he'll return any money you've paid him for his services—a remarkable guarantee from a health-care professional.

After running more tests, he told me, "While you have high calcifications of the coronary arteries, that doesn't mean you're going to have a stroke or heart attack because your inflammatory factors are low." According to their philosophy, although I had the disease, it wasn't active.

Because Dr. Bale lives in Nashville, Tennessee, travel became difficult, especially during the pandemic, so I began to see a team of doctors who had a similar philosophy at Yale New Haven Hospital. They recommended a stress test, which I passed, scoring in the top fifth percentile of fitness for someone my age. However, during the stress test the ECG was slightly abnormal and a tracer they injected suggested low blood flow to a portion of my heart. A coronary computed tomography angiogram (essentially a noninvasive test in which the coronary arteries are imaged by a CT scan and blood flow to the heart can now be estimated) was subsequently performed. The test showed that I had calcifications in my coronary arteries and that my left anterior descending artery, what is often referred to as the widow-maker, was completely blocked. Additionally, a major branch of that artery was significantly blocked.

At that point, I called my friend Dr. Zarich and sent along my test results. It was a Saturday, but he reviewed the images electronically and passed them along to two of his colleagues immediately. Within an hour, they had all read my results. Their consensus?

I had nothing to worry about—at least not immediately, because clinically I was extremely well compensated. Rather than running to the hospital, I could simply come in for a regular appointment on Monday. Two days later, I was discussing my case with Dr. Ari Pollack, a cardiologist that Dr. Zarich has recommended, who assured me that, although I had calcifications and blockages in a portion of my left anterior descending coronary artery, I still had good cardiac function and performance. My body had likely compensated, thanks in large part to my dedication to health and fitness for all those years. "But," he told me, "If you want to be sure, get a coronary angiogram, and a stent could be placed if that is deemed to be necessary." Then he gave me his cell phone number in case I had any questions or concerns.

Within ten days, he had set me up with Dr. Robert Fishman—another cardiologist, and one of the best in his field—who coincidently had cared for my father fifteen years prior. Soon after, my angiogram was scheduled, and I had Dr. Fishman's personal number tucked away in my phone as well.

How often do doctors give you their personal numbers? How frequently do they stop what they're doing to review your test results on a weekend? I told the doctors responsible for my care how much I appreciated their attention and how unusual I found it to be. All of them had the same response: they did it because they loved their work. And they knew that, even though scans like mine were something they saw every day, it was a big deal to me. It was important to them to make me feel comfortable—just as important, in fact, as it was to do a good job with the procedures themselves. My doctors let me know I could call them anytime, day or night, and continued to text me regularly to check in.

I was told to show up at the hospital at 6 a.m. on the day of my procedure, and I was escorted to a room as soon as I arrived. The nurses provided excellent care from the moment I got there, and the whole team came in to say hello before I was wheeled into the operating room. In the room itself, everyone was positive and enthusiastic—I couldn't imagine being more relaxed in a hospital environment.

Dr. Fishman's findings were exactly as he had expected: by eating well and working out for my whole life, I'd done my own bypass, feeding blood vessels called collaterals from another healthier artery. There was only a minimal decrease in blood flow to my heart, despite the fact that my "widow maker" was 100 percent blocked. My right coronary artery had compensated, and a new branch had formed. Two stents were placed to open things up, and immediately the doctors saw a positive change on the CT, indicating an increase in blood flow.

After the procedure, Dr. Fishman came in to tell me what he and his team had found and what they had done. He was thorough and kind, and I expressed my gratitude.

Soon after, I returned to Dr. Pollack's office. He assured me that everything had gone well and asked whether I had any questions, letting me know that I had a full thirty minutes of his time. "I want to make sure you feel comfortable," he said. I later learned that the group of doctors I had seen were known for providing excellent customer service, and my experience reflected that reality.

Todd Williams, one of the leading hospitality consultants for Four Seasons Hotels and Resorts as well as Centura Health, states, "Today, you've got to be exceptional." In a health care climate in which it's very difficult for patients to find a doctor that is not only competent but also compassionate, it's an effective way to differentiate yourself from the competition.

Treating large volumes of patients to bring in money and offset costs may seem like a viable option. However, I believe this is a mistake. Being a competent, technically trained doctor is necessary and important. **Ultimately, it's about the care—and kindness—you provide.** Doing the best you can for your patient at every turn is the only way to be truly great.

Go Above and Beyond

By now you know how important the service aspect of any interaction is in business. With that in mind, going above and beyond when it comes to the patient experience—and the service you provide—can be a vital element of your success. In my practice, we keep a list of what we call "the little things," small touches that make a tremendous difference in the service we provide (you'll find them in the book's Appendix).

Ultimately, we aim to offer an extraordinary experience that feels more like a trip to the spa than a dental examination, with numerous amenities available from the moment patients arrive on site. There is ample parking, free of charge, and our facility is handicapped-accessible, to assure no one has difficulty entering the building. Although COVID-19 precautions have altered our approach, there are typically fresh fruit, juices, a selection of teas, and Starbucks® coffee—both regular and decaffeinated—in the waiting room, along with thirty different magazines.

The bathroom is pristine and stocked with toothbrushes, toothpaste, mouthwash, floss, Williams Sonoma® soaps, luxe hand creams, and a sign that reads, "We take pride in keeping our clinic clean for our valued patients and guests. If this facility is not in tip-top condition, kindly alert any team member."

Our private care rooms—equipped with aromatherapy, digital music systems with a vast song collection piped through personal headphones, warm towels, and lip moisturizer—are another way we set ourselves apart. These details may seem small, but they make a tremendous difference in the way our patients feel. That, I've learned, is priceless.

Summary: Rebuilding the Doctor-Patient Relationship through Service

We've discussed the ways in which the monetization of medicine has damaged the doctor-patient relationship. As practitioners, it is our job to repair it. Many little things go into providing an excellent experience—some of which we've covered in the previous chapter—and most are quite simple. In some of the most uncomfortable medical situations I've endured, a simple check-in from the doctor or team member, during the procedure and after its completion, would have made a world of difference.

In this day and age, when so much is determined by what insurance companies will and will not cover and how much they'll pay, doctors often worry about how much time they are spending with patients—whether in the examination room or over the phone. They fear they will lose money if they linger for too long. But as Darrell Cain, founder of Cain Watters and Associates—a financial services firm catering to the dental industry—so wisely explained, **"Care more about the value you create than the money you receive. People will stand in line to hire you, and the money will come."**

Providing a Patient-Centric Experience

- Above all, it is your job to make the patient feel cared for. Doing so not only puts them at ease and increases the likelihood that they will return but also reduces their stress—which has a significant impact on overall health.

- Don't be overly concerned about the money; invest time and energy in providing the best quality patient experience you can, and the rest will follow.

- When evaluating the kind of experience you provide, think back to the best and worst experiences you have had as a patient and adjust accordingly.

- Then, do your best to go above and beyond, exceeding expectations with your offerings. Ultimately, it's *the little things* that make the biggest difference.

Questions to Consider

- Is your approach to patient care and follow-up based on providing the best quality experience or on compensation?

- What have your experiences as a patient taught you about providing care?

- Describe your best experience as a patient and as a customer. Observe the similarities. Observe the differences.

- Describe a less-than-ideal experience you may have had as a patient. What could have improved it? How did it make you feel?

- Do your policies and practices reflect those lessons?

- Are there certain businesses both within and outside of health care that you frequently refer people to?

- What influences your decision to make a strong referral?

- What small, low- or no-cost changes could you make to improve the patient experience today, tomorrow, and for years to come?

- What could be preventing you from instituting them?

6

The Walking Wounded

Cultivating Human Connection and Preventing Disease in a Disconnected World

When I was a child, my mother taught me a powerful skill that became the basis of my professional approach and a key element in achieving my life's purpose. She taught me how to connect with others.

My mother, Joanne Sonick, worked in real estate for William Raveis. With a photographic memory and a knack for making anyone and everyone feel comfortable and safe, she was a natural. In the morning, she could help someone navigate Section 8 housing in some of the poorest parts of Bridgeport, Connecticut. In the afternoon, she might show waterfront property in Southport to a multimillionaire client. She would undoubtedly treat both clients with the utmost kindness and respect, creating the kind of rapport that brought her many referrals and repeat customers. My mother could truly relate to anyone.

Tell Patients the *Why*

People like my mother draw others in. We enjoy being around people who can cultivate mental, spiritual, and physical connection. That ability goes much farther than technical prowess in any field. If I were to tell patients only about the *how* behind their treatment—eliminating pockets, drilling holes, placing screws, applying bone and growth factors, and so on—I would lose most of them right away. When I tell them the *why*—that my treatment plan will make them feel better, look better, eat better, and communicate better, that they won't have to worry about losing their teeth or feeling pain, that their lives will be more joyful—I lay the groundwork for connection and trust.

That approach feeds *my why*, to improve the quality of people's lives, and helps to fulfill the mission of my practice: to improve patients' lives through education and motivation in a comfortable, caring, and friendly environment. That practice mission statement, developed with seven of my team members in a hotel conference room in Mystic, Connecticut, back in 1988, is as elemental to my operation today as it was more than thirty years ago when my team and I created it.

The Types of Doctor-Patient Relationships

Regardless of whether connection is key to your mission statement—personal or professional—it is an essential piece of creating enduring and effective doctor-patient relationships. To understand why connection is so crucial, we can begin with the different types of relationships we can have with our patients.

In his book *Being Mortal: Illness, Medicine, and What Matters in the End,*[27] surgeon, writer, and public health researcher Atul Gawande describes three types of doctors: paternalistic, informative, and interpretive. In *paternalistic relationships*, like those cultivated by old-school physicians, the care provider is the authority. They typically don that white coat, hand down a diagnosis, and instruct patients on what to do.

Many of those in my parents' generation—who came of age during World War II—were traditionalists. They valued those paternalistic relationships, respecting their doctors automatically and doing what they said without question.

But doctors are not all-knowing. We are just human beings who have cultivated a particular skillset. And in truth, there is no way to gauge a doctor's skill just by looking at them, or even by reviewing their files.

When it comes to professional athletes, we track their successes and failures—the percentage of times they make a jump shot when the game is on the line, for instance. But no one knows what percentage of the time doctors are correct in their diagnoses. We just don't keep that kind of data. That means that much of what patients have to go on is internet research, word of mouth, and how a doctor makes them feel.

Many doctors believe themselves to be the ultimate authority. They bestow their diagnosis and treatment plan on a patient and expect them to listen, as though they were a parent instructing their child not to eat ice cream so close to dinnertime.

Doctors working to foster an *informative relationship* take a slightly different tack, providing a bit more information and options and allowing the patient to make a decision. An informative dentist might say, "So, Al, you have decay in this tooth and an abscess at the root. We could do a root canal, a crown lengthening procedure, and place a crown, which will take about four months. Or we could take out the tooth, do a bone graft, and place an implant and a crown, which will take a bit longer. What would you like to do?"

Rather than hearing from one's parent that it's not quite time for ice cream, this experience is akin to dining at a pretentious restaurant in your neighborhood and receiving a menu in a different language, or one that is rife with words you cannot understand and ingredients you've never heard of. Although the doctor may provide more information, it's often still not enough for the patient to confidently make a decision. Worse, the patient may feel uncomfortable during the process—preventing them from understanding much at all.

The best doctor–patient relationship is what Gawande calls *interpretive*. It requires a shared decision-making process. The doctor provides the risks, benefits, and costs of each of the choices. This is an experience not unlike grabbing dinner at a favorite restaurant with excellent service. Your waiter is kind and down-to-earth and fosters a sense of ease. In an interpretive relationship, the doctor is not the authority and the patient is not the child. They are at the same level.

Provide Everything Patients Need to Make an Informed Decision

In 1994, my mother died of colon cancer, which had metastasized to her brain, at the age of sixty-four. After her doctors found that the cancer had spread, they gave her the choice of whether to have chemotherapy. But they did not tell her that her chances of living more than six months were less than 15 percent.

Without that vital insight, she chose chemotherapy. In the span of just four months, she went from being a relatively vital woman to a shell of herself. The chemotherapy destroyed my mother's quality of life without extending her longevity by much—if at all. Had they given her a full picture of her options and the risks and benefits of each, she might have made a different decision.

Of course, that decision is far more significant than whether to try to save a tooth, but the concept is the same. Oftentimes, dentists tell their patients, "We can try to save the tooth," and nothing more. The patients agree to try, because it seems like the best option. Who doesn't want to save their natural teeth? But if the patients knew that the process would require multiple procedures and that the success rate would be somewhat low—with a high price tag to boot—they might choose differently.

That's why, in my practice, I allow the patient to drive the bus. My job is to be there with a decipherable map. My job is to inform and educate patients about their treatment options. Knowledgeable patients are better able to choose the right course of care for themselves.

> I allow the patient to drive the bus. My job is to be there with a decipherable map.

The Right Kind of Connection

Today, there are fewer paternalistic doctors out there. That's due in part to the fact that patients are savvier than they used to be, with more access to information thanks to the internet. As a result, doctors tend to be informative, giving patients choices as to the course of their care. But very few are interpretive.

Although they require relinquishing some of your power, interpretive relationships are best for both doctors and patients. Research has shown that patients who play a role in their treatment decision-making process actually heal better, because they have more control over their experience. In a world marked by so much uncertainty, being able to provide some of that control, along with comfort, love, and, of course, connection, is a gift for both parties.

Cultivating that interpretive relationship takes time. You cannot rush through a packed schedule of patients and expect to earn their trust and forge a bond with them. In fact, slower medicine may be one beneficial outcome of COVID-19. We cannot process as many patients in a day because of social distancing restrictions and the need to wear so much more protective gear, so we have more time to spend with the patients we do see. And that means we have more opportunity to connect. Regardless of the societal conditions under which you're reading this book, consider whether it's time to slow down and think through every step of your process.

What's Your Process?

By the time I meet with a patient, they have already had at least five or six interactions with my office. Most of my patients—about 60 percent—are referred by other dentists. Friends and family members refer most of that remaining 40 percent. Those referrals count as interactions because they have the potential to affect a patient's perception of what I can offer them.

Furthermore, approximately 70 to 80 percent of people today read reviews online and visit a doctor's website before making an appointment; thus, most patients have likely explored our website before walking through our doors: their second interaction. They have also spoken to our receptionist to make an appointment over the phone (which a live person always answers by the second ring): interaction number three.

By the time they are in the examination chair, they have met with my administrative team and been greeted by name on arrival (interaction four) and have connected with my dental assistant in the examination room (interaction five). All of these interactions must be positive so that the patient feels comfortable providing all necessary information before I arrive.

By the time I enter the room, my team has identified the patient's chief complaint, retrieved or acquired the person's dental and medical histories, and taken a full-mouth series of x-rays and photographs of the patient's teeth—all of which a team member enters into our system digitally. The interactions serve to provide me with the data I need but also ensure the patient feels heard and nurtured from the moment they begin engaging with our practice.

I review all of the data before stepping in for the initial examination, which is probably the most important hour I spend with a patient over the entire course of treatment.

When I arrive, I sit down across from them, "knee to knee, eye to eye" as Dr. Robert Levine, my close friend and fellow periodontist, says and practices. Then, I introduce myself—inviting them to call me *Doctor* or *Mike*, depending on what they prefer (traditionalists often go for the former, and millennials typically choose the latter).

My only goal here is to remove barriers to treatment and show them that I'm on their side, that we will be working together to solve their problem. And, thanks to Malcolm Gladwell, I know that I only have sixty to ninety seconds to make that all-important first impression (or sixth impression, as is the case here).

I tailor my approach depending on the patient's presentation. Knowing that what people say composes a very small portion (approximately 7 percent) of what they convey to others, I observe all of the ways they communicate—body language, tone, pacing, and more.

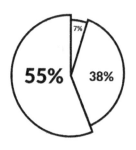

Mehrabian's "7–38–55 Rule" of Communication"

7% - The words
38% - The voice
55% - The face

Mehrabian, A. (1972). Nonverbal communication. Aldine-Atherton, Chicago, Illinois.

Then, I use a technique called "mirror and lead," matching their tone and body language to create a sense of familiarity, and then using *my* tone and body language to guide them. For example, if a patient is gesticulating wildly and speaking rapidly, I'll do the same and then slowly lessen the breadth of my movements and the pace of my language until we are both interacting calmly. If a patient won't make eye contact with me—as is often typical with teenage boys—I'll look away too, talking to the wall and attempting to catch their gaze every once in a while until they begin to focus on me. Why? If they are calm and comfortable, they are more likely to feel as though they have control over their future.

I also use another effective gauge: a pulse oximeter, which measures one's pulse in addition to oxygen saturation. That pulse is another indication of how they're feeling. If it begins to increase, I can tell their anxiety is creeping up. If it's high—around 110, for example—I'll work via mirror and lead to bring it back.

Based on what I learn in those first moments, I do my best to make them feel comfortable. Sometimes, that comes in the form of a well-timed joke; other times, it's simply listening to all they have been through.

Ultimately, I know that what I do as a doctor is of almost no consequence. It's about getting a patient enrolled in their own healing process, alleviating the stress they may be feeling, and affirming that they have the agency to get better. As practitioners, we must remember: the body is the hero, not us. Thus, **it is our job to help the body and mind do what they were built to do: heal.**

Regardless of how they behave, most patients come in afraid, a barrier to healing. Why? They're grappling with the unknown: *How bad is it? How much will it hurt? How much will it cost? Will the state of my mouth cause me embarrassment and humiliate me?* That unknown makes them anxious, as anxiety is essentially a reaction to fears about the future. **I have to convey to them that they are in a safe space here and now, and that it's going to be okay.**

Often, I'm not even sure what I'm going to do yet when I reassure them. Still, I know that in the end it will indeed be okay. Why? I've committed to making it so. I've been doing this long enough that I'm familiar with most of the solutions out there, and if I can't fix it, I will find someone who can. In dentistry and beyond, virtually every problem has a solution.

To ensure patients know I can solve their issue, I explain exactly what's going to happen. I start by asking permission to examine their mouth—an essential element in any care environment. They usually say yes. However, on occasion they will not be comfortable with an examination right off the bat. If that is the case, I do not judge but ask them to come with me to a nonclinical area where we can just talk. After the examination, I explain what I found, offering the patient a mirror so that I can point out what I'm describing if they'd like to see for themselves. My staff and I always ensure for our patients that all the information on the computer screens in the room is visible to them. This often aids in taking away some of the mystery that can make a doctor's visit so nerve-racking.

Another motive behind deliberate choices like these? Making sure I have informed consent. Patients must be aware of everything that will happen, every step of the way. Providing a clear and detailed explanation—in a manner they can understand—enables us to achieve that. That brings me to the foundation of my approach: education.

Educating the Walking Wounded

My average new patient is about sixty-five years old. Most of them have been seeing dentists their whole life. As a result, many have spent thousands of dollars and hundreds of hours in the dental chair on dentistry that may have been done poorly or failed to hold up over the years because of a lack of maintenance and care. By the time they see me, they're often dealing with an emergency. Most of the time, it's not that they haven't spent the time or the money to handle the problems they've had. It's that no one has taken the time to explain to them what's happening in their mouth, what they need to do to fix it, or how to take proper care of their teeth. I call them the walking wounded, and I help them understand what they've been through using what I call "the Sonick Curve."

The Sonick Curve is based on the Jellinek Curve of Addiction, which Dr. Elvin Morton Jellinek, a Yale physiologist and a pioneer of addiction science, developed to explain the trajectory of alcoholism.

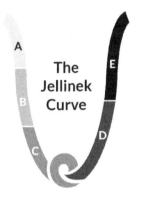

A. PROGRESSIVE PHASE
Use turns for relief and tolerance develops

B. CRUCIAL PHASE
Use increases and problems emerge

C. CHRONIC PHASE
Problems mount and control disappears

D. REHABILITATION PHASE
Abstinence begins and help sought

E. RECOVERY PHASE
Life improved and hope restored

The top left-hand side of the curve represents the risk of falling into addiction. The bottom of the U-shaped curve represents the throes of addiction. Those there have hit rock bottom and have likely lost functionality and connection in numerous areas of their lives, including jobs and relationships.[28] That curve has a trapdoor: death.

However, a program provides the potential for mental and physical rehabilitation. People can make their way to the top right-hand side of the chart, as long as the addiction hasn't caused irreparable damage.

The Sonick Curve is also U-shaped.

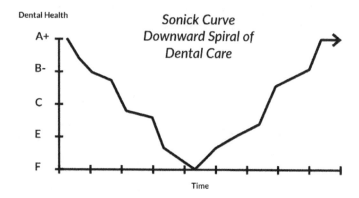

The top left-hand side represents the teeth one is born with, before the ravages of dental disease: periodontitis, trauma, and decay. Almost everyone has a nice complement of teeth to begin with. Over time, the issues rack up. A patient may get a filling during childhood. Soon, they need a larger filling—and eventually a cap. Then a crown. Then a root canal. Then an extraction. The list goes on.

To illustrate their issue, I draw the Sonick Curve and show them where they fall. Then I tell them that if they become a patient in my office and follow my advice, they will never get any lower on the curve. Their freefall into dental destruction will cease.

"I can stop you from going downhill," I say. "I can't tell you for sure that I can get you back to the top, but I can get you close—and I can certainly prevent you from sliding farther backward. Depending on how fast you want to proceed, it may take months or years. But together, we can stop the decay, the disease, and the bone loss." That is a powerful picture, and you can paint it too.

Charles Revson, one of Revlon's founders, said, "In the factory we make cosmetics; in the store we sell hope."[29]

What I'm giving patients is more than a diagnosis or a treatment plan. I'm giving them hope and a solution.

I also tell them that to be successful, I'll need their help. "Are you willing to do that?" I'll ask.

"What's it going to take?" they often reply.

> **What I'm giving patients is more than a diagnosis or a treatment plan. I'm giving them hope and a solution.**

"It's going to take showing up at my office when I recommend you come in for treatment—and being here on time, paying our agreed-on fee, following a few steps at home, and getting your teeth cleaned every three months for the rest of your life. Otherwise, I can't help you," I tell them.

This process is called co-discovery, and it is almost identical to the one designed by Dr. Bob Barkley.

Lessons in Prevention from Dr. Bob Barkley

Robert F. Barkley was born in 1930 and grew up in Ipava, Illinois, a town of 600 people. After attending Northwestern University Dental School in Chicago, he returned close to home, practicing in Macomb, Illinois, just over twenty miles from his hometown. He died at the age of forty-six in a small plane crash on the way home from a speaking engagement.

In his short life, Bob had a tremendous impact on our field, pioneering the concept of preventative dentistry. Early in his career, he realized that the techniques he had learned in school were failing, so he decided to change course. While his peers in the 1950-60s would often practice "extension for prevention," making fillings bigger than they needed to be and inadvertently making patients' problems worse, Bob took a different approach, eventually providing more education and less dentistry with the goal of "making the patient worse at the slowest possible rate."[30]

To do that, he realized he needed to work with the patient to teach them about their problem and the possible solutions, make a joint decision about how to proceed, and make a commitment to the path ahead—together.

In his own practice, he engaged in a process he called co-diagnosis, in which he and the patient would identify the problem and arrive at the solution as one. To facilitate this collective effort, he never reviewed models or x-rays before a patient's arrival. Rather, he would "think out loud" while the patient was in the chair, because he found that to be the best possible method of educating them. "I am more concerned about teaching you how to prevent dental disease than I am about repairing it, even though I make my living by fixing teeth," he said.

He was also unsurprisingly a big proponent of connecting with patients. Just before his death, he had been planning to write a book titled *Humanistic Dentistry*, which would explore humanistic psychology, relationships, and how they could be applied to our field. Over the course of his brief career, he had learned just how much humanism mattered. When I learned about Bob, I felt as if I'd found my philosophical twin.

Today, few dentists and physicians provide the kind of education that Bob did and that I offer in my office today. They don't teach patients how to brush and floss properly, perform a diet history and monitor what they eat, advise on proper exercise, or measure their daily amount of sleep because there isn't a billable code associated with it. But education is the only way to help patients understand their diagnosis and options for treatment, make a decision that is in their best interest, and commit to doing everything necessary to maintain the work you will do together.

Breaking It All Down

Many dentists claim they practice preventative dentistry, but that's rarely the case. Rather, they practice procedural dentistry.

My practice breaks down treatment into two parts: preventative—or hygiene—in which patients see a dental hygienist to prevent issues and maintain their oral health with regular cleanings, and active treatment, in which we conduct procedures to get patients healthy. At the completion of active treatment, patients move to the prevention portion of our practice, the hygiene room.

My goal is to get all our patients to the hygiene room. Prevention is at the core of what I do. There is no need to treat disease if it is prevented. With that in mind, let's break down the four phases of all treatment. These phases apply not only to dentistry but to medicine, architecture, agriculture, or any problem in need of solving. I call these phases the Treatment Checklist.

Prevention is at the core of what I do. There is no need to treat disease if it is prevented.

1. Examination
2. Diagnosis
3. Treatment plans
4. Active treatment

There are also five protocols that fall across the four phases of treatment:

1. Elimination of pain
2. Control of active dental infections

3. Functional rehabilitation
4. Aesthetic dentistry
5. Maintenance

I share the four phases and five protocols with patients on the first visit. I also tell them that on that first visit, we're going to do an examination and diagnose the problem(s). I let them know that they'll receive a diagnosis along with some treatment options, but that we won't be doing any treatment that day.

The only time treatment is performed on the initial visit is when the patient is in pain or has a severe infection. In that case, I'm attending to that first protocol—elimination of patient pain—and only when it's an emergency. Even then, I do the minimal amount of treatment necessary to get them comfortable. When in pain, the only outcome a patient desires is to be pain free. At the conclusion of this initial visit, patients are urged to return for a comprehensive discussion as to what their long-term options are for establishing and maintaining long-term health.

I want our patients to be completely informed before care is begun. Patients should never have buyer's remorse. A patient should be committed to their own long-term care and prevention if we are going to achieve the kind of outcome we're looking for.

After the comprehensive examination, all patients receive a letter that reviews the diagnosis and their treatment options. The letter serves as a written record of our conversation and also allows patients to think about their choices, discuss their options with any loved ones, do more research, and feel confident about the treatment plan we develop together. It is also part of providing exceptional care. Rarely do patients receive a personal letter from their doctor. It is informative and takes the mystery out of treatment. I frequently tell my patients that I am pulling back the curtain and letting them see what's backstage, like in *The Wizard of Oz*. I have found that with knowledge, fear is often reduced. In fact, I believe that the antidote to fear is knowledge.

The antidote to fear is knowledge.

Next, I control infection or disease; primarily periodontal disease (infection of the gums), decay (infection of the teeth), or trauma (like a baseball or fist to the mouth). This phase may also involve care from other specialists, such as an endodontist for a root canal or a restorative dentist who can take care of decay.

Once the infection is under control, patients come back for a reevaluation visit. This serves as an opportunity to plan the next phase: functional dentistry. Functional dentistry covers the stuff most people think of when they think about dentistry—braces, crowns, implants, etc. But it's crucial that we don't move on to that step until a patient is pain- and infection-free.

During that reevaluation session, I sit down with the patient and give them all of their options. With functional dentistry, my goal is to segmentalize the issues and only address what is essential so that we can improve on the dentistry in the future.

Cosmetic elements may be a part of the functional dentistry we do as well. When everything is complete—their mouth is healthy and free of infection and I've done only the procedures necessary to get them well—patients move into the maintenance phase.

Maintenance may include cleanings twice, three times, or four times a year. It may involve using fluoride every day or a special mouthwash once a month. It may be wearing a bite guard at night. Regardless of what it entails, each maintenance process is custom-tailored to the patient.

Most important, patients must understand that maintenance is ongoing. Decay and periodontal disease are chronic and incurable, just as is the case with diabetes, hypertension, coronary artery disease, alcoholism, and obesity. That's why getting patients to commit to care up front is so important. The reality is that only about 15 percent of patients comply—as is true in dentistry and medicine at large—but 100 percent of them get the information they need for proper maintenance. We put it in writing, as well, both before the course of treatment begins (as I mentioned) and after the functional dentistry is complete. That way, they can never say they didn't know maintenance would be required.

Ultimately, it's prevention, and thus, maintenance—scaling and root planing and oral hygiene—that are the cornerstones of a healthy prevention-oriented practice. If a patient has good oral hygiene (which we teach them over the four to five one-hour visits they have with a hygienist if they come in for scaling and root planing), I can say with a high degree of certainty that they won't lose any teeth. Treatment—and maintenance—enables us to stop periodontal disease in its tracks. But it does require that patients show up every three months to get their teeth cleaned and that they brush and floss on a daily basis.

Most dentists, and physicians as well, don't push maintenance; they push treatment. Why? It's where they make their money. But guess what? Doing the right thing doesn't hurt the bottom line. Patients should not be scared into treatment. They should be told the truth. Our practice is booked out months in advance by doing what is necessary and in the patients' best long-term interest. Why do we do the right thing? Because it's the right thing and it works well for both the treating health-care providers and the patients.

A Holistic Approach

As you develop a process for educating and treating patients, keep in mind that the best dentistry is no dentistry at all. I can never make a tooth as good as God does. With that in mind, I try to get patients healthy so that they need as little dentistry as possible now and in the future. And that requires a holistic approach to health.

In their book *Younger Next Year*,[31] Chris Crowley and Dr. Henry S. Lodge discuss how adults fifty or older can become "functionally younger every year" for the next five to ten years, living as if they are in their fifties even in their eighties.

To do so, individuals must follow these four simple rules:

1. Exercise six days a week.
2. Eat what you know you should.
3. Connect to other people.
4. Commit to feeling passionate about something.

Many of their guidelines align with the four elements necessary to maintain good health: sleep, diet, exercise, and mindfulness.

With that in mind, when I first meet with patients, I ask them to complete a diet history, writing down everything they eat for four days—from Thursday through Sunday because I want to see what they eat over the weekend. Only about 30 percent of patients send it back. When they do, I review it, looking for hidden sugar.

Why? As you know by now, only that which we measure can we improve. If I don't measure or evaluate what they are eating and drinking, I cannot help them improve. And in many cases, there is sugar hiding where they least expect it. It may be in the ketchup they put on their burgers, or in the mint they suck on before bed, or in the daily Coke they have around lunchtime. When I know where that sugar is hiding out, I can help patients find and avoid it.

Plus, we don't just do dentistry; we're a health-care practice. That means we must attend to the other factors that contribute to overall health, because they are necessary to treat the whole person.

There are very few patients who come into my office in their eighties and carrying around 150 extra pounds and with a bad infection. Why? Those who aren't healthy just don't live that long. Dentistry gives me the opportunity to motivate patients to be healthier and thus live better lives.

My friend and former colleague Dr. William MacDonnell experienced my approach firsthand—albeit with a bit more tough love than I typically offer my patients.

Bill and I worked together every week for decades. He was my dental anesthesiologist and an excellent one. His care contributed to the comfort of hundreds of my patients. He has a kind, gentle, empathetic demeanor that immediately puts all patients at ease. He struggled with his weight. Food was his drug of choice, and when the going got tough, he relied on it to make it through.

After losing his wife and supporting his four children on his own, his health began to decline swiftly as his weight increased. That same year, he had a stroke. I consider Bill one of my closest friends, and I was very concerned about his health.

One day, I asked him whether we could talk. "Do I need to hire another anesthesiologist?" I asked him.

"Why?" he replied.

"Because the way you're going, you'll be dead soon," I told him as I handed him the book *Younger Next Year.*

That dose of tough love was meant to get him to address an ever-growing problem, and it served as a wake-up call to Bill. He read the book. He lost one hundred pounds and has kept it off for more than a decade.

Today, Bill works out every day. He has a new girlfriend. He's retired, not because of his inability to work, but of his own volition. And now he's spending his newfound free time with his family and volunteering in his community. He's living life on his own terms. Most important, he's happy—and in the best shape of his adult life.

As dentists and doctors, we have the chance to help people live their best lives—regardless of our specialties. **To do that, we must connect with them as people, focus on prevention, and address every part of their being—rather than reducing them to parts.** Caring for the whole person, rather than our bottom lines, is the way to cultivate true success for them and for ourselves.

> Caring for the whole person, rather than our bottom lines, is the way to cultivate true success for them and for ourselves.

Summary: Earning Trust, Commitment, and Consent through Connectivity

Connecting with your patient is fundamental to your ability to meet their needs and put them on the path to healing. Although we may like to think it's our hands that do the most important work, the patient's body and mind are actually responsible for that particular miracle. After all, if you were to perform a procedure on a patient who died shortly thereafter, no healing would occur.

Although it may hurt our egos a bit, we must realize that we are not all-knowing; rather, we are just human beings who have cultivated a particular skillset. Our work should reflect that. **The goal should always be to build a trusting relationship with the patient, through which you can both determine the right course of action.** Thus, it is up to you to make sure the patient feels comfortable, to reduce stress—which can interfere with healing—clarify what they can expect, and gain their commitment.

Doctors and patients should be in the treatment process together, with the patient stationed confidently at the wheel. Because connection is key to this process, you must consider the experience you and your team provide. Is everyone the patient interacts with personable and prompt from the moment they call your office, or must they wait on hold for four minutes just to make an appointment? Does your team take pains to put them at ease, or do they feel neglected, rushed, or even inconsequential during those interactions?

When you arrive, what do you do to make them feel seen and heard and to assuage their worries? What do you do to earn their trust?

Remember that, when you take the time to explain their case and get their buy-in, you're not only cultivating connectivity but you're also giving patients hope.

Note, too, that the best thing you can do for patients is help them *prevent* disease rather than just treat it. Addressing the whole person and ensuring they know their part in directing their care will enable them to partner with you in ensuring their own well-being now and in the future.

As Bob Barkley explained, somewhat tongue in cheek, our goal as practitioners should be to make patients worse at the slowest possible rate. Focusing on human connection helps you do just that.

Fostering Connection Every Step of the Way

- Regardless of whether connection is key to your mission statement—personal or professional—it is necessary to create enduring and effective doctor–patient relationships.

- According to surgeon, writer, and public health researcher Atul Gawande, there are three types of doctor-patient relationships: paternalistic, informative, and interpretive. Today, most of them are informative. All of them should be interpretive.

- As practitioners, we must remember this: The body is the hero, not us. Thus, it is our job to do our best to ensure the body and mind can do what they were built to do: heal.

- Remember that education is key. We must inform and educate so they can make the best decision for them.

- Treat the whole person, not just the problem at hand.

- Focusing on prevention is the right thing to do. And because patients will trust you and refer friends and family, doing the right thing never hurts your bottom line.

Questions to Consider

- What is your *why*? Will working to cultivate connections with patients and others in your life bring you closer to fulfilling your life's purpose?

- Have you considered the role of connection in your work previously?

- How can you adapt your approach to better connect with patients?

- What does your process look like? Are there parts you could refine or enhance to paint a clearer picture for patients and help them commit to their treatment—without experiencing buyer's remorse?

- How do you educate patients? Is there more they need to know? Is there more *you* need to know to provide them with better care?

- Do you practice the four phases of treatment (exam, diagnosis, treatment plans, treatment) on every patient? If not, why not?

- What are the five protocols of treatment? How do they apply to your practice?

- Is the protocol different for a patient presenting in pain than a new patient to the practice who is pain free?

- Does the philosophy of Bob Barkley make sense to you?

- How could you incorporate co-diagnosis into your practice?

- What changes would you have to make to practice the four phases of treatment?

- What's your perspective on prevention? How is that reflected in your practice?

- Does your discussion of patient health only include the mouth or your specialty? Do you provide patients with a comprehensive list of other professionals that could also help them to become healthier?

- Do you write a letter of your findings and treatment recommendations to every patient in your practice? If not, why not? Would you consider it?

- What one change might you make today to make you a better doctor?

7

Hire Slow, Fire Fast

Building a Team That Will Work for You and Your Patients

E very morning, without fail, the first thing I do as I walk up the stairs to my office is close my eyes. In that moment, everything I've been thinking about—the traffic on the short drive, a stressful conversation, even a particularly delicious breakfast—fades away. My only goal is to get into the proper mindset so that I can fulfill my role.

In every organization, each person holds a specific role—sometimes more than one. Our team is no different. In our practice, I am a surgeon and I treat patients. I play a part in educating others in my practice and beyond. I am involved in our marketing approach. And of course, I lead the team and help guide our vision. But I know I'm no more important than anyone else in my practice, nor are my practice partners, my office manager, my dental nurses, creative director, or my hygienists. Our success requires that everyone fulfills their unique responsibilities every day.

And one of my roles is ensuring that we have the best people for the job and that they are equipped to fulfill the roles they have taken on. To do that, my team and I, like many of the world's best companies, hire slow and fire fast—vital advice from leadership and business strategist Greg McKeown.

Take the Time to Make the Right Decision

I once spoke to a young dentist who had just completed the interview process for a new job. His prospective employer had spent two to three months poring over his materials, interviewing him, and vetting his references. Then they told him they would hire him to work in the office for one day a week.

"Only one day a week?" the dentist asked, trying to hide his incredulity.

"Yes," the hiring manager replied. "If one day works out well, we'll bring you on two days a week. Then three, then four, until you're here full time. If that goes well, we'll make you a partner."

The dentist asked me why I thought they were spending so much time onboarding him. I told him the process was good for both of them. They would be able to determine whether he was a good fit for the practice, and if not, both parties would be free to move on. That's a win-win in my book.

Tony Hsieh, former CEO of Zappos, employed an interesting tactic as part of the company's slow-hire strategy. As an organization dedicated to not just satisfying customers but wowing them, Zappos trains new hires for four full weeks on its unique culture, strategy, and approach to extraordinary customer service. A week into the training, new employees receive what the company calls "The Offer": if they quit right then, they will receive payment for the amount of time they have worked plus a $1,000 bonus.[32]

Why would Zappos do such a thing? Tony and his team knew that if new employees took them up on the offer, they weren't the right fit for the company and its high-touch, customer-centric culture.[33]

Prioritize Practice Culture

My team and I take a similar approach when it comes to prioritizing practice culture. We are there to open doors for our patients, not close them. We never say "no" to a patient (though we may tell them, "We'd love to be able to do that; however, we've tried in the past and it just didn't work out well," a statement that essentially accomplishes the same thing—all while appeasing the person in the chair). **Creating that culture requires us to have the right people on board and in exactly the right seats.** Those who can't provide that kind of experience just aren't for us.

I started out as a party of one, and today, I have a team of over twenty people on board who are absolutely essential to what I do. Without them, I couldn't practice at the level I do. And each of them embodies our unique culture and appreciates and upholds our values. I would happily live next door to every single one of them.

Patients come and go; I've probably seen over thirty thousand over the course of my career. But good team members tend to stick around. Some of my team members have been with me for more than twenty years, and I am well aware that they are not obligated to stay.

In fact, I consider my employees volunteers. While they get paid, they work in our practice by choice. They can leave at any time; they are not indentured servants. Oftentimes, members of my team receive offers for more money to move to another job. Time after time, they choose to stay because they like the environment and culture our practice provides. They believe in our mission—to improve the quality of patients' lives—and it's important to them to work in a place with a purpose similar to their own. I ensure those that I bring on board think similarly.

Hiring the Right People—and Treating Them Well—Pays Off

In winter of 2020, I offered a woman we will call Sofia an office management position. Her position at another organization had recently been eliminated, and she was anxious to find a new role. Ours would require slightly more responsibility than her previous job, so we offered her a bit more money than she had asked for. She thanked me for the offer and told me she would think about it.

That weekend, she unexpectedly got another offer, which would pay even more than we would. She asked whether we would match it, explaining that she had a lot of financial responsibilities, and the additional funds would help her meet them.

My team and I had a decision to make. Would we match the amount the other organization was offering or let her go? Ultimately, we decided that the rate she was requesting wasn't affordable.

When it comes to hiring—and to seeking a position—money isn't the only factor. My team and I knew about the other medical office offering her a job. The organization had a very different philosophy from ours. Rather than being patient-centric, it focused on production and procedures.

My office manager cautioned her about the environment, explaining that she had been a patient there, and that she thought Sofia wouldn't be happy with the experience. Still, she told her she understood her financial commitments and wished her well. Having spent days vetting her, and believing she'd be a great addition to the team, she also asked Sofia to contact her if things didn't work out at the other office.

Less than two weeks later, Sofia called. She was already very unhappy in her new role and believed working there challenged her integrity. We ended up offering her the position again and agreeing on a slightly higher rate than what we had originally proposed. She put in her two weeks' notice at the other medical office, and we scheduled her start date for March of 2020.

Then COVID-19 hit the Northeast United States. On what was supposed to be her first day of work, we closed our office with no idea when we'd be able to open again.

My partner asked me what I wanted to do.

"We could furlough her, but that would create financial hardship. If we pay her while the office is closed, she'll see that we are extremely loyal to our employees. And I have a feeling she'll show us the same kind of loyalty."

We agreed to pay her. The office remained closed for the next two-and-a-half months. But with Sofia's help, we accomplished so much. We refined our marketing and social media channels. We created a TV studio on the second floor of our building and began running weekly Zoom meetings on preparing for the future of our industry for over two hundred dental professionals across the globe. Together, we built a reputation as a dental practice and educational center that was there as a resource for other practices all over the world during one of the most challenging periods in our lives.

Deciding to hire Sofia and keep her on full time the day we closed our practice was one of the best decisions my partner and I have made—for us, for our teammates, and for Sofia herself. And it's a testament to the value of a good hiring process, and to hires with great character.

Do You Have the Right Fit?

Typically, I know whether someone will be a good fit for the practice right off the bat—regardless of their experience. My longest-running employee, Liz, has been with me for over two decades. I knew she'd be a good fit when we hired her. She was working in Bridgeport at Chaves Bakery—the purveyor of those great Portuguese rolls—behind the counter, providing excellent customer service. Today, she is my right hand, a phenomenal dental assistant who is responsible for the clinical inventory, ordering, and the office's maintenance and repairs. She handles it all flawlessly.

One of my newest hires, Dr. Stephanie Koo, is a young periodontist who will eventually become my practice partner. She earned her undergraduate degree at Brown University and completed her dental training at Harvard. I knew I wanted her to join me three years ago when she started her residency at the University of Connecticut School of Dental Medicine, where I've been an instructor in the postgraduate periodontal program for more than fifteen years. I appreciated the way Dr. Koo carried herself. Her appearance was polished and professional. Unlike many young residents, she always looked me in the eye. She was confident and direct but never pushy.

I told my wife, Carole, right then that I thought Dr. Koo would be a good fit for the practice, and that I wished I didn't have to wait the three years until she graduated to hire her. I ended up waiting just two years before making an offer. When I asked her whether she was interested in joining the practice, she didn't hesitate to say "yes." Just as I was impressed by her presentation, she told me she appreciated what my practice had to offer, including the chance to continue teaching and learning and our focus on providing ideal treatment.

Shortly after I brought Dr. Koo on board, I received confirmation that I had made the right choice. I asked her how she would like me to introduce her to the community. "Would you like me to introduce you as my practice partner?" I asked.

"No," she responded, "I don't feel comfortable with that. I'm not your partner yet, and I don't want to lie." In that moment, she demonstrated a character trait I check for throughout the hiring process: integrity. In business, like life, integrity is everything.

Hiring Advice from a Leading Grocery Business

Stew Leonard, Jr., is a patient of mine. His father founded Stew Leonard's, which began as a small dairy store in 1969. Today, it's a nearly $500 million business—a six-store supermarket chain with locations throughout the tri-state area and more than twenty-five hundred employees. Its excellence in customer service has earned it a spot in *Fortune* magazine's "100 Best Companies to Work for in America" list for ten consecutive years.

The company's dedication to customer service and employee satisfaction is apparent. When I visit a Stew

Leonard's, everyone who works there seems to be in a good mood. If I have a question about where to find a particular product—say, a bunch of bok choy—they don't just tell me where to find it; they walk me over to the bok choy. The experience is akin to the check-in process at a fine hotel like the Ritz-Carlton, during which a staff person often walks you to the elevator and provides you with your room key at that time.

One day, I asked Stew Jr. how the company trained its employees so well.

"Well," he said. "We show everyone a twenty-minute video my dad made about twenty years ago, and then they go to work."

In that moment, I realized that, rather than having an exceptional training process in place, Stew Leonard's had a way of finding the right people. Of course, they had instituted protocols—including a process for onboarding new team members that was undoubtedly more detailed than what Stew shared with me. But more than anything, the company found people who embodied the traits they valued from the start. We do the same.

Dental hygienists have to go to school for four years before they begin cleaning teeth. Dental assistants typically train for nearly a year before staffing a practice. But they inevitably bring their approach to treating people with them into that training, and into the positions that follow. Thus, our goal is to find people with traits that serve our mission, vision, and values. **We can always train them on the technical stuff. It's far more difficult—if not impossible—to teach them how to be kind.**

How We Hire

With that in mind, although none of our hiring assessments check for intelligence, a number of them gauge characteristics—such as the integrity Dr. Koo showed when she turned down my offer to introduce her as my practice partner.

In my practice, applicants complete an online form with basic information about their professional experience, as well as the Culture Index survey—a personality inventory we use as a pre-screening tool. It was first introduced to me by visionary Michael Hall, who delivered an inspiring presentation on human analytics at a financial meeting hosted by Cain Watters. Before the meeting, all of the audience participants were required to fill out the Culture Index survey. At the end of the lecture, Michael asked whether he could share the survey results of a few audience members with the group, mine being one of them. Armed with only a ten-second reading of my Culture Index survey, he gave an extraordinarily accurate assessment of my personality in front of four hundred people without ever meeting me. I was impressed. It was eerie how accurate he was.

The Culture Index is a survey, not a test. There is no passing or failing, nor is there such a thing as a perfect result. The survey doesn't measure intelligence or one's learning ability. It doesn't determine race, gender, religion, age, or anything clinical. Rather, the exercise gives us invaluable insight into a candidate's work-related behaviors and whether they may be effective in the position for which we are considering them.

We take the Culture Index results so seriously that we won't interview a potential employee or even look at their resume until we receive and review their Culture Index. It's so important that we refer back to it even after we hire the candidate. Everyone's Culture Index results are displayed on their desk, so that members of the team can understand each other's work style and communicate about it at any time.

Once the prospective employee completes the Culture Index, the hiring coordinator reviews the results and conducts a quick internet background check, including a review of personal social media profiles (Facebook, LinkedIn, Instagram, and others). If there are no obvious red flags, the hiring coordinator shares the information with me.

If I think the candidate looks like a good fit, we schedule a ten-minute FaceTime® interview, during which the coordinator runs through a series of questions on everything from the candidate's ability to their working style, professional interests , and hobbies. The questions enable us to gauge whether they are interested in working with us based on our culture—and that cultural alignment is essential.

Why? More than anything, every member of my team, from the front desk staff to my periodontist partners, must be able to make patients feel comfortable. They must be able to meet patients where they are—which is often a place of fear—and alleviate their anxiety. To do that, and to contribute to the calming, solutions-oriented culture we have established, they must display the traits of compassion, a strong work ethic, and curiosity. Furthermore, they must align with our core values of health, integrity, education, and being servant-hearted, and team-oriented.

Throughout the process, the candidate inevitably reveals a number of tells as to whether they're the right fit for the role and for our practice culture. If the first question they ask is "What's the benefits package like?" or they haven't taken the time to look at our website, chances are they don't care about the environment in which they work—and aren't very curious.

The next step is a fifteen- to thirty-minute in-person interview with our team. Of course, any interview is an opportunity to put one's best foot forward. If they show up five minutes late to their interview, they probably won't be on time for a regular day at work. The same goes for one's appearance. Uncombed hair, chipped nail polish, and dirty shoes tell me that they don't really care about their appearance. In a health care environment, where cleanliness is of the utmost importance, that's an automatic out.

During the interview, I always come in for a *Blink* moment—a short and sweet encounter that provides me with a meaningful first impression. I do a quick scan of everyone I meet—hair, eyes, smile, fingernails, clothing, and finally, shoes.

Then, I evaluate their eye contact and their handshake. Do they look at me directly? Is their grasp firm and confident? Combined with their timeliness, that helps me develop an impression in a matter of moments. Sometimes it only takes sixty to ninety seconds to make a decision about whether to move on. Simultaneously, whether they know it or not, potential hires are conducting their own *Blink* test on me. It is equally important that I and my team make a good impression as well.

What Kind of Impression Do You Make?

Dr. William "Bill" MacDonnell, whom I mentioned in the previous chapter, had been my anesthesiologist for years when he decided to retire. He is also one of my closest friends.

Bill is a born connector, a great man who wants to make everyone happy. His work ethic so aligned with our mission, vision, and values, that I bought him a pair of white sneakers to keep in the office and put his name on our sign and on our website, even though we worked together only one day a week. When he began to dial back his practice, my anesthesia cases decreased as well—from about one hundred per year to just five or six annually.

When he decided to retire for good, he introduced me to a young anesthesiologist who could take his place, a nice young man whom I will call Dr. Jim.

Dr. Jim is brilliant. He speaks three languages fluently. He is well trained and attended the most prestigious training programs. However, he struggled to connect with our team members. His appearance and approach sent a message that wasn't doing him any favors. For one thing, he did not wear spanking clean white sneakers like the rest of the team.

One day, he came to see me. "You're very successful," he said. "Who do you use for marketing?"

Anyone can hire a marketing company to draw attention to themselves, but that in and of itself won't make them successful. Joe Polish, founder of Genius Network®, is considered one of the most influential connectors of entrepreneurs in the world. He says marketing is putting people in front of you. According to my coach, Dan Sullivan, Founder of Strategic Coach, selling is something entirely different. He says, **"Selling is getting someone intellectually engaged in a future result that is good for them and getting them to emotionally commit to take action to achieve that result." Marketing is irrelevant if you cannot sell, and that requires connecting.**

"I don't really use anyone for marketing," I told him. "My team creates my content."

"Bill told me you were good at marketing," he said.

"My team and I are good at *connecting*. I can tell you have trouble with that."

"Yes, I do," he responded.

"You're someone who would rather just think and plan than connect," I noted. He nodded.

"You can overcome that," I said. "How much business do you want?"

"I don't know."

"Don't you think you should know that before you start marketing?"

"Yeah," he said.

"How many cases have we done together?" I asked him.

"None," he said.

"That's right. How many cases did Bill do a year?"

"I don't know; maybe four or five hundred?"

"How many did he do with me?"

"I don't know."

"Look, you're smart. You're kind. You're empathetic. You're a brilliant anesthesiologist. But that's what everyone expects. When I go to a restaurant, I expect that the meat I order won't be contaminated. I expect the dishes to be clean. People don't come to see you because you are a brilliant anesthesiologist; they come to see you because they like you. I like Bill MacDonnell. I liked him before we became good friends. I put his name on the sign. In fact, it's still there. I don't want to take it down even though he's retired, because I like him so much. His white sneakers are still in the basement.

"What if I told you my practice made up 25 percent of Bill's income?" I continued. "What if I told you that another 10 to 15 percent of the business he did was based on referrals I made directly to him?

"Let me tell you who you need to market to. You need to market to me," I finished.

Then I asked him whether he was willing to be mentored. He nodded.

After finishing one of our first cases together, he asked me how he'd done.

"Very well," I told him.

"What could I have done better?" he asked.

"Well, clinically, nothing—it was perfect."

"Great," he said.

"But there is one thing..."

I stood by the door and waited for a staff member to walk by. The first person to approach was Karen, who runs my front desk. She had been with me for five years at that point, and she knew our culture quite well. In fact, she exemplifies it daily by her uncompromising commitment to providing each and every one of our patients with a great experience. She unfailingly goes above and beyond. And that is what exceptional teams and practices do—not occasionally, but every day. I asked Karen to step into my office.

"Dr. Jim, would you mind standing up for a minute," I asked. He did. I could see that he was nervous. "Karen, can I ask you a question?"

"Okay," she said.

"Look at Dr. Jim. What two suggestions can you give him?"

She looked down at his shoes but stayed quiet. I could tell she didn't want to hurt his feelings.

"It's okay," I told her.

"The sneakers," she said finally.

"What about them?"

"They look about five years old—like something you might want to wear while working on a boat. They should probably be white."

"Anything else?"

He had what looked like two weeks' worth of facial hair that he'd just let grow in, no trimming, no shaping—nothing.

"You need to shave," she said.

I thanked her and she left. Dr. Jim looked confused.

"Do you think your appearance is important?" I asked him. "Karen noted it immediately. And everyone in the office noticed it too. Do you think they're going to go out of their way to schedule a patient with you if they don't think you look professional? Don't you think you would be more successful if you had this whole team on your side? You won't be a better anesthesiologist if you shave or wear white sneakers, but you will be a more successful anesthesiologist. And you will have better relationships."

Dr. Jim didn't say much. He seemed to be taking everything in.

I called him four days later, just to make sure he was okay after our big talk. "How are you doing?" I asked.

"I'm doing well because I just bought some white sneakers. Can I leave them in your office?" he asked. "I don't want them to get soiled by wearing them out of the clinic."

"Of course, you can," I told him, and I smiled to myself. I knew I'd gotten through.

Today, Dr. Jim has a very busy dental anesthesia practice. So busy, in fact, that we must pre-book his time months in advance.

Key Questions

Of course, my evaluation doesn't end with someone's appearance. I ask them a few things based on their resume and Culture Index. Then, I always pose the same question: *What annoys you the most in a work environment?* Their answer provides keen insight into whether they will struggle or thrive in ours. Answers range from the commute to the pay, coworkers' tendency to gossip, and a lack of organizational integrity. This question usually leads to an emotional reaction. When someone reacts emotionally—either positively or negatively—it offers a window into the person's consciousness. That paves the way for a more open conversation and a better connection. Once they've opened up about what bothers them, they're more likely to share insight into their personal and professional experience—as well as what they can and can't bring to the table.

Typically, it's the next question that tells me whether they are truly interested in what we do: *Have you been to our website?*

If they say "no," they're probably not going to be hired—plain and simple. The same goes for those who say they have been to our website but cannot tell me anything about our practice. In short, it shows a complete lack of curiosity or interest—nonnegotiable traits in our practice.

I'm also listening to see whether they gossip or talk about others, including their current or previous employer. Those who do are all but guaranteed to do the same if we were to hire them, making gossip another automatic disqualifier.

We invite those who pass this phase of the interview back for a three- to four-hour working interview day, during which they'll shadow the administrative and clinical members of the team.

And because my team is essential to my success, I value their opinions above all else. If even one person doesn't like a particular candidate, that person won't move on to the next phase of the hiring process.

The candidates who pass that phase will complete the Clifton Strengths Assessment, which outlines their top talents. There are a total of thirty-four themes. Individually, each theme will give you an indication of what you naturally do best. For example, according to my assessment, I am an achiever—I have a constant need for achievement; a learner—I love to learn; and a realtor—someone who thrives on genuine relationships. I'm also intrigued by individualization, or the unique qualities of each person, and I tend to take charge.

We also have candidates take the Kolbe A™ Index, which measures the instinctive ways in which people take action. The results describe a person's natural strengths, their modus operandi. This assessment aids us in determining whether an individual is a good fit for a particular role, in addition to whether they will align with our culture.

Finally, when we're satisfied that we have the right person for the job, and after a background check, we bring them back to hire them in person. During that meeting, we present them with a written description of their duties, the hours they'll work, and the benefits package they will receive. If they are happy with the package we've presented, they'll sign on the dotted line and schedule their start date.

It may seem like a hassle for everyone involved, but having a thorough process ultimately saves time and money while providing peace of mind. I know everyone on my team has the skills and drive to accomplish what needs to be done, and I know that new hires will likely be satisfied with their roles as well.

Summary: Hiring Someone You Can Count On

Every organization's success is dependent on whether its team members can fulfill their roles. That makes hiring crucial to your strategy. To ensure we get it right, my team and I hire slow and fire fast (and ideally not at all), taking the time to vet each candidate thoroughly—from first impressions to qualitative assessments.

In health care, employee appearances set the tone for patients, conveying to them that they are in a clean, safe atmosphere just as much as an immaculate waiting and examination room do. They also highlight an individual's attention to detail. Thus, those who arrive at an interview looking unkempt rarely move on to the next phase of our hiring process.

Character is also key. While I can educate a staff member on techniques and protocols, they must already embody traits such as integrity. With that in mind, I look for those innate elements when making a hire.

Because I know that my team members are absolutely essential to the work I do, they have the final say. If someone isn't a fan of a particular candidate, we don't hire that person.

Although taking such pains with your hiring process may seem excessive, there's nothing more important than the people on your team. As such, finding the right ones must be a priority.

How to Hire for Fit

- Character is essential. With that in mind, evaluate innate traits when considering a new addition to your team.

- The Culture Index provides a clear picture of candidates' values and how they typically perform at work, thus providing valuable insight into whether someone will be a good fit for a particular role—and for the team at large.

- In this case, appearances—and first impressions—matter! A neat and clean appearance and a timely arrival indicate that your candidate pays attention to the details.

- Your team's happiness is essential to success. Thus, their opinion on a potential hire matters.

- Don't rush. The process may feel tedious, and you may worry that you're asking too much of someone, but having a thorough process helps ensure the right fit for both parties.

Questions to Consider

- What is your mission, your *why*?
- Does your culture and those you've brought on board reflect it?
- Does everyone in your organization know your *why*?
- When employees are not functioning well, it is usually a result of a misfit with the core values of the team. Does your organization have a set of core values?
- Are they written? Can each of your team members articulate them? Do you verbalize them to potential candidates during the hiring process?
- What is your current hiring process?
- Do you have a written protocol for hiring?
- Would you consider using evaluations to find the right employees?
- Do you work with a group of unique individuals who function as a team?

- Do you have the right people in the right seats?
- Can some of these people change seats in your organization to deliver better results?
- Have you been happy with those you've brought on board? If not, could a better process help you eliminate the wrong people for the job?

8

Unsung Heroes

Cultivating an Effective Team Culture

Let's talk about one of the greatest football teams of all time: the New England Patriots. The Patriots have won six Super Bowls, and Tom Brady, who spent the first twenty seasons of his NFL career with the team, was there for all of them (he played in nine Super Bowls during his tenure as a Patriot). He's since won yet another Super Bowl with the Tampa Bay Buccaneers.

Brady is a phenomenal quarterback. You might even say he's the great surgeon of the team. But he wasn't the only one responsible for building it. Coach Bill Belichick might say that he had a hand in that. He was the team's visionary, assembling the players and dictating the plays.

And while Brady shone on the field, he wasn't more valuable than any other members of his team. If he threw a touchdown pass to win the big game, no matter how perfectly executed, if the tight end wasn't there to catch it or dropped the ball, the team wouldn't win.

The highest-paid player on most teams is the quarterback, but often the second highest-paid player is typically someone anonymous to everyone but that quarterback: the left tackle. Why? The left tackle protects the right-handed quarterback's blind side when he drops back into the pocket and is looking for receivers. If someone hits the quarterback, he can't make that touchdown. Worse, if he gets injured and winds up out for the season, it could cost the team millions of dollars, or even be life threatening. As such, the quarterback must be able to trust that the left tackle will block any player that comes his way. That makes the left tackle an unsung hero and one of the most important members of the team.

No Player Is More or Less Important than the Next

Thus, no player, coach, or teammate is more important than the next. And it's crucial to remember that as you build, train, and support your own team in your dental or medical office. In my practice, the clinical team members who ensure I have the proper sterilized equipment to operate, from scalpels to suction and gauze, are just as essential to any one procedure's success as I am.

Here's another example of why no team member is more or less valuable than the next, this time in a dental office rather than on a football field. Before I begin a surgical procedure, I often grab a pair of latex gloves. Most of our patients—99 percent—are not allergic to latex. I always check the patient's chart, but I don't think much before reaching for a set of latex gloves. It's my assistant's job to double-check the patient's chart and ensure they're not part of the 1 percent. If they are, there's a protocol in place. She removes all the latex gloves from the room and replaces them with nylon ones so that I can't make a mistake.

My team is ensuring I'm set up for success in other ways too, even before I meet with a patient. The first thing a teammate does before I walk across the threshold of the operatory is state the patient's name, their procedure, the medications they take, and the tooth, quadrant, or area of the mouth on which we are operating. I will repeat after them, double-checking the chart and x-rays. *I'll* restate the information, and they'll repeat it back to me once more. (For more on the importance of checklists, check out *The Checklist Manifesto*[34] by Atul Gawande, which highlights the importance of using checklists like the ones we employ in daily professional life.)

The redundancy of our process is intentional. Patient safety is of the utmost importance. Running through a checklist of these crucial factors—and repeating them—is essential to keep patients safe. That is our ultimate priority. On graduating from medical and dental school, new doctors take an oath of ethics attributed to the Greek physician Hippocrates. The most important statement of the Hippocratic oath is *primum non nocere*, "first do no harm." With this as one of our guiding principles, we repeat information and adhere to checklists to avoid doing harm.

My teammates are also watching closely as I begin to administer the anesthetic, ensuring that I'm administering it to the correct side of the mouth. That's a mistake I don't make, but having someone there serves as a backup who can keep me on track. **Put simply, it's every member of our team's job to make the others better.**

Before we get into the ins and outs of our day-to-day operations, we must address the bigger picture: our philosophy.

What's Your Team-Based Philosophy?

As I mentioned in the last chapter, my team is more important than my patients. Without an excellent team, I cannot provide the highest quality service, and I cannot help patients get better—my ultimate goal. And one way that I ensure I have the right people on the team, and that we can all support each other to success, is through our philosophy and shared values. Your philosophy must be known and practiced by everyone in the organization—not just the leadership team. The people who repair our equipment, paint our walls, pick up our trash, cut our lawns, run our marketing campaigns, and provide service directly to our patients, from answering the phones to cleaning their teeth, all share the same philosophy. We are dedicated to improving lives, one patient—one person—at a time.

I consider myself a servant leader. Yes, I provide the vision and I sign those checks, but I do it in the service of my team and my patients. I know that I receive more by giving, and so does the rest of our team. And we run our office with that philosophy—helping others and helping patients get better above all else—in mind. The philosophy I bring to work is no different than the one I bring to my relationships with friends and family and to every person I meet. Being a doctor is not who I am. Being a doctor is what I do to help others. I search for teammates who take the same approach.

Building a team with the same philosophy does take some time. Hiring, as you learned in the previous chapter, is the first step. I try to bring on other selfless servants, people who want to help others by nature. In doing so, I know that I'm building a team of individuals who will readily share in my philosophy.

Put Those Protocols in Place

With our philosophy squared away, we look to another essential element of successful team operations: protocols. I'm the practice owner and surgeon, but I don't run the office. The protocols, backed by our philosophy, do. Therefore, it's crucial that the protocols are crystal clear.

And thanks to those protocols—from how we onboard new patients to the way we proceed with an examination—I don't tell people what to do. The protocols inform the way we move forward. Furthermore, each member of my team is accountable for their role and the tasks assigned to them, and for holding others accountable as well. **Every person on my team has permission to tell another teammate if they are not doing their job properly, if they're making a mistake, or if something needs improvement. In fact, they're required to do so.** If we want to operate successfully, members of the team cannot cover for each other when someone deviates from the protocol and makes a mistake. That would prevent us from identifying the origin of the issue and keeping it from happening again. And in a medical environment, mistakes can prevent us from being able to conduct procedures; they can even be deadly.

It's that individual and collective accountability that ensures our practice operates efficiently, effectively, and—above all—safely.

We cannot be accountable without protocols. Protocols help us standardize our procedures, from the way we order supplies to the way we schedule appointments and perform surgery. Although no one on the team is exactly the same, it's crucial that we do things in the same way and that the protocols dictate our approach.

We have nine dental assistants on our team. They are all well-trained and operate according to our documented standardized procedures. Ideally, there should be no difference in their individual clinical performances. It's not unusual for me to think Danielle is assisting me during a procedure, only to look up and find Liz or Sarah by my side.

If two members of our team responsible for the same types of tasks are handling them differently, we talk about it and compare strategies to find the best way forward. **We must set aside ego for the good of the team.**

Take our oxygen supply, for example. If we run out of oxygen one evening and have a surgery scheduled for the next morning, we can't do the surgery. Without oxygen, we cannot perform anesthesia.

Because oxygen is so essential, we keep three backup oxygen tanks to prevent us from ever running out. We almost have to go out of our way to run out of oxygen. If that mistake were to occur, multiple team members would be responsible for the oversight, because various individuals are in charge of checking the tanks. And if every one of those people covers for the others, we won't find out where the issue began, preventing us from developing a protocol that could resolve the problem going forward.

Instead, we rely on our individual and collective accountability to get to the bottom of an issue. **When an unforeseen problem occurs, we ask four questions:**

What happened?

Why did it happen?

What can we do so it doesn't happen again?

What have we learned from it?

To return to our oxygen example, we may find that someone realized the tanks were low and failed to communicate that to the person responsible for ordering more. With our answers in mind, we can alter the protocol to build in fail-safes that will help us avoid a similar outcome. Perhaps we could make more people responsible for checking the oxygen, or we could incorporate a procedure for follow-up so that the person responsible for ordering knows to check in with others if they haven't heard anything after a set period of time.

And while covering for other members of the team only hinders our ability to be excellent, we must be accountable for each other in a different way as well: by having each other's backs. To be clear, that doesn't mean hiding others' mistakes; it means picking up the slack when it's necessary. If someone is sick, for instance, or unable to come into the office for another reason, the rest of the team steps up without hesitation. Teamwork is one of our five core values.

Conveying a Uniform Message

Meanwhile, our synchronicity goes beyond philosophy and protocols. We all have the same goals, the same ethics, the same attitudes. We speak to patients using the same language. Those are the elements of synchronicity that patients pick up on.

Most of the patients who come to see me don't know about our international reputation. They don't know that we've been practicing for more than thirty-five years at a very high level. They don't know that I lecture residents at the University of Connecticut, have been on the faculty of Yale School of Medicine, or that I've taught at NYU College of Dentistry since 1984. They're unaware that I lecture internationally, edit industry journals, and have written my own textbook. But they know that the office is spotless. They know that the team is cohesive and that every member is kind and helpful. They know that we are all perfectly coordinated in our uniform—jade scrubs and, you guessed it, white sneakers.

Other practices take a different approach. The administrative team may wear business casual, while the clinical team is in scrubs, and the doctor dons a tie and white coat. In our practice, everyone looks the same—doctors, hygienists, dental assistants, IT and marketing staff, and receptionists all wear the same scrubs. It makes us appear unified and ensures patients know who is a member of our team. The same goes for the New England Patriots, and for every sports team out there, and that's because wearing the same uniform makes a real difference. It makes everyone feel unified in multiple ways.

When we are wearing the same uniform, there is no hierarchy; everyone is held to the same standards. Most importantly, we *feel* like a team in our scrubs, and when we're wearing them, we're reminded that we all adhere to the same philosophy and protocols. It's another element of standardization that makes us incredibly effective together.

> When we are wearing the same uniform, there is no hierarchy; everyone is held to the same standards.

Build Something Greater than Yourself

Our outfits aren't the only way we maintain coordination. We start each morning with a team meeting that sets the tone for the day. We go around the room sharing what we call "Something Sweet." Team members offer up something sweet that has occurred in their life recently, or a moment they were particularly proud of in the office and beyond.

We also take time to acknowledge each other. The practice has more than thirty-five hundred five-star reviews online. When a patient mentions an assistant or hygienist by name in a review, our marketing manager will post the review on our website and immediately share it with the whole team. Almost daily, the team receives an email recognizing a colleague. It makes everyone feel as though they are participating in something greater than themselves, and that's the key to work satisfaction.

Yes, our patients pay us for the work we do. Nobody would show up if they didn't receive an income in exchange for their efforts. We all have mortgages, bills, tuition, and more. But all of us work for a higher purpose. That's truly why we show up each day, and it's why we show up for each other.

People want to be part of something greater than themselves. Because our philosophy and our team provide that opportunity, it's very rare that someone leaves for another job. If they are great, and they align with our values, we invest in their growth in numerous ways, offering opportunities for personal and professional development and promotion. With support and acknowledgment like that, there's rarely a reason to leave.

We also recognize their worth financially. The pay rates we offer are among the top 5 percent of our industry. We provide a phenomenal benefits package, which includes pension planning, continuing education, and other intangibles—including parties, staff outings, and our annual trip to New York City.

Each summer, we take the train into the city and spend the day doing things members of the team may not have ever experienced before. We might start with a tour of Grand Central Station, or a boat ride in Central Park. Then, we might sail around Manhattan on a ninety-foot sailboat as the only passengers aboard. Next, we might head to an escape room, before having a catered dinner at a five-star restaurant. For four of the five most recent excursions, we've had dinner at one of Danny Meyer's restaurants, followed by a Broadway show.

One year, we took the team to see *Kinky Boots*. The musical director, Will Van Dyke, is the son of the head of my residency program at Emory—Dr. Tom Van Dyke, one of the world's leading authorities on immunology and periodontal disease. Tom is also my academic mentor and teacher, as well as a good friend. I've known Will since he was three. Before the show, I called Tom and asked whether Will would be willing to meet my team after the show. He agreed.

The show was amazing. It won six Tonys. Afterward I told the team I wanted them to meet the musical director. After the theater cleared out, he came onstage and invited the whole team to join him. Looking out across the empty theater, I knew it was an experience none of us would ever forget.

Our annual excursion is a costly day for the practice financially, but the expense is entirely worthwhile. It's a real privilege to be able to share some of the things I love about the city with my team. Just as my team goes out of their way to give patients a "wow" experience, I go out of my way to do the same for them. Of course, my commitment to them isn't limited to rewards for excellent service; it's reflected in the way I lead, coach, and mentor.

Constant, Gentle Pressure

I like to conduct experiments in my office. From time to time, I've stopped playing my role on the team in various areas. I've stopped mentoring or stopped leading altogether. Occasionally, that happens naturally, like when I go on vacation for a few weeks. Other times, I do it purposefully. During the COVID-19 pandemic, I worked in the office three twelve-hour days a week. We split the team into two separate units so as to avoid unnecessary exposure. One day, I said to myself, *I wonder what would happen if I just came to work, treated my patients, and went home?* I did that for two weeks. What happened was remarkable.

In a few short days, I felt as though I had arrived at a different practice. A stain appeared on the carpet and remained there for days on end. Part of the fence fell down. A leak sprung up on the second floor, and no one mentioned it for two days. Light bulbs went and stayed out. No one changed the air filter in the basement.

These are simple things, but because of the lack of communication and leadership, everyone thought someone else would take care of them. Ultimately, it's up to me to keep things running, to be the cheerleader urging the team on.

Danny Meyer shared an important lesson he learned about management from Pat Cetta, the owner of Sparks, a New York steakhouse. Danny was in his twenties at the time and told Pat that he was struggling to send his staff a consistent message.

"If you choose to get upset about this, you are missing the boat, luvah," Pat told him, and then, as Danny wrote, "he gave me a demonstration that has become integral to the way I view management."[35]

He had Danny take everything off the set table next to them except for the saltshaker, and to leave the shaker by itself in the middle of the table.

Then, he asked Danny where the shaker was.

"Right where you told me, in the center of the table," Danny responded.

"Are you sure that's where you want it?" Pat asked.

When Danny looked closely, he could see that the shaker was about a quarter of an inch off center.

"Go ahead. Put it where you really want it," Pat said.

Danny moved it to the center.

Then, Pat pushed it three inches off center.

This continued, with Pat instructing Danny to move the shaker back to center, before moving it a few inches off again.

Finally, Pat told Danny,

> Listen, luvah. Your staff and your guests are always moving your saltshaker off center. That's their job. It's the job of life. It's the law of entropy! Until you understand that, you are going to get pissed off every time someone moves the saltshaker off center. It's not your job to get upset. You just need to understand: That's what they do. Your job is to just move the shaker back each time and let them know exactly what you stand for. Let them know what excellence looks like. And if you're ever willing to let them decide where the center is, then I want you to give them the keys to the store. Just give away the f—in' restaurant![36]

That lesson helped Danny establish and teach a managerial style he calls "constant, gentle pressure—it's the way [he] returns the saltshaker to the center each time life moves it."

Every team, no matter how great, requires that constant, gentle pressure to stay on track, and if you're the leader of any operation, it's your job to provide it. Regardless of how much you empower your team—which you should do—if there's no visionary pushing the team to the next level, you'll find yourself stuck or backsliding.

Some teams may be good without it, but I don't want a good team; I want a great team. If you want to reach an elite level, you must be firing on all cylinders, all the time. There's no room for misses, whether that constitutes something as significant as a misdiagnosis or as minor as a bad mood.

If you lead with a partner, you must be on the same page when it comes to constant, gentle pressure and every other element of your practice. I'm fortunate to have an excellent partner. We're not the same person by any means, but we are both on the same page, and that makes us an effective team.

We do play two different roles as leaders, however. You'll remember the concept of showtime and being on stage whenever your practice doors are open. Well, there are also backstage and front-stage responsibilities.

There's the stuff people see—what happens on stage during showtime—and everything that occurs behind the scenes. When patients come to your office, they don't see the inventory system, the chart write-ups, the sterilization process. They don't see the team of twenty-two people that coordinates every aspect of their experience. My partner manages many of the backstage elements, taking care of management, ordering supplies, and scheduling. Meanwhile, I'm front and center, serving as the face of the practice. And that's not the only difference in our roles.

Every Team Needs a Visionary

A cohesive unit that operates like a well-oiled machine doesn't just establish itself; it takes a visionary to build it. In our practice, that's my role. Note that a visionary is not a *boss*. It's someone who defines the practice's mission statement at the outset and is responsible for constantly bringing energy to the business and team so that vision is carried out. That differs from my partner's role. We do share some responsibilities—we are both surgeons, we both see patients, we both do treatment planning—and we carry out those responsibilities in an almost identical manner for the sake of standardization, but that Visionary® role is mine alone.

In their book *Rocket Fuel: The One Essential Combination That Will Get You More of What You Want from Your Business*, authors Gino Wickman and Mark Winters talk about the importance of execution.[37] Integration—taking the protocols established by the Visionary, leader(s), and team and distributing them to the people accountable for them—is essential to building that well-oiled machine. The Integrator® takes the vision and transforms it into reality. I may, for example, hire speakers and choose dates for our regular study club, but my role stops there. Someone else does the integrating: booking the venue, ordering catering, sending out contracts, communicating with our IT staff, posting the information on the website, and sending out marketing material to our network to make sure participants fill the room when the day arrives.

Every team needs a Visionary, an Integrator, and executors to accomplish the tasks at hand. Raymond Kroc was McDonald's Visionary. He took the McDonald brothers' idea—and the nine franchise locations they had opened—and created a global franchise that would become the most successful fast-food corporation in the world. Meanwhile, Harry Sonneborn was Ray's Integrator. He had an idea: What if Kroc owned the land McDonald's restaurants were built on and then leased the land to each franchise? The

"Sonneborn Model" is often lauded as the most important financial move in the company's history. Today, McDonald's real estate holdings constitute 99 percent of the company's assets and 35 percent of its revenue.[38]

In my practice, Integrators incorporate my vision into the administrative, hygiene, clinical, marketing, business, and physical aspects of the business. We also have a backup Integrator in case the primary Integrator in any one area can't handle it. For example, Liz is responsible for all our ordering. If Liz can't do it for some reason, Detuan will handle it. Sarah runs our lab work. If she can't do it, Danielle or Lexy will take over.

Ensuring It All Gets Done

How do I ensure everything gets done and maintain strong relationships with my team? A former resident of mine, Dr. Sejal Thacker, is now program director of the periodontal residency program at the University of Connecticut School of Dental Medicine. She manages residents and faculty at the university, as well as at her private practice. She is brilliant at what she does and has a great commitment to the residents and to her patients. And like all of us, she faces the challenges of running an organization. One day she asked me, "Dr. Sonick, how do you manage your team? You can't be their friend and you can't be their boss."

"Well," I responded, "I'm probably neither. I approach them as another human being sharing my experience and vision with them. If they align with what I'm offering, great. I invite them to join me. If not, I tell them I understand, with the knowledge that they are probably not a good fit for my practice—and that's okay too."

I haven't always taken that approach. Early on, I would come into a team meeting with a list of edicts on what I needed done. I'd roll through them quickly and move on. But eventually, I realized no one was listening to my laundry list of decrees. What do people hear? The message behind it all.

As such, today our meetings are very different. We work together to strategize. Rather than make demands, I share ideas, asking how we should handle a particular problem. And together, we determine the best path forward. I've also learned when to let go of certain tasks.

There are thousands of processes in our office, from ordering equipment to seeing patients and maintaining the building. Our organizational chart clearly specifies who is responsible and accountable for all tasks. I'm responsible for a very small number of them. Rather, it's my job to ensure the various people in our organization take care of them. And I'm very careful about how I do that. Micromanaging would only add more to my plate—taking me away from my real responsibilities—and disempower my team. I take a different tack, empowering my staff to do their jobs. If I see that they're having problems, I don't hesitate to step in and provide the coaching they need.

Know When and How to Coach

A while back, I hired a very bright teammate named Taylor. She earned a master's degree at a top college in New England. When she had been with us for a year, we conducted her annual review. As part of the evaluation process, the team member fills out a four-page survey, grading themselves on various aspects of their role on a 0–5 scale.

Taylor gave herself threes across the board. According to her, she was average at everything. Taylor is not an average employee. I knew that, regardless of the way she'd filled out the document. But I could see how hard on herself she was, and that critical lens was holding her back.

"I see some blockages preventing you from getting to the next level, and it's not because you're not bright," I told her.

"I just don't think I'm good at this," she replied.

"I know," I said, "I saw your review. It's one of the worst I've ever seen an employee give herself. You're an A-employee who gave herself a C review."

As we went through her review together, she mentioned that she was struggling with numerous aspects of her role, one of them being time management.

I shared with her a process I had learned from Dan Sullivan at Strategic Coach, the Four Cs: commitment, courage, capability, and competence.

"Will you commit to improving your time management skills?" I asked Taylor.

"I don't know if I can," she said.

"The reason most people don't commit is because they are fearful. Making a commitment requires courage. Everything I've ever done in my life that had any real value required courage—from learning to ride a bike at age four to placing my first dental implant at age thirty-two.

"Even today, I get a little nervous before a procedure because I've committed to doing it in an ideal manner. I get a little nervous before I lecture or give a presentation, even though I've done thousands of them. And I appreciate the nerves, because they keep me fresh. But it's courage that keeps me going and allows me to commit.

"So, are you willing to commit, and do you have the courage to do it?" I asked.

"Yes," she replied.

"Well, once you do that, you will develop capability in a new area. Do you have any capabilities now?"

"I do," she said tentatively.

"Taylor, do you think you are intelligent?" I knew the answer.

"Yes," she said.

"Do you think you're more intelligent than most people?" She hesitated, her modesty holding her back.

"Tell me the truth," I prodded.

"Yes," she said.

"So do you think you can learn time management?"

"Yes," she said.

"Well, how about this: I know you can. And if you commit to it, I will mentor you through it."

"I commit," she said.

"I've actually been trained in time management. Thirty-five years ago, I took my first time management course, and I've been working on it ever since."

I gave her some simple strategies to address it and told her we'd work on it together.

At seven that night, I got the most beautiful letter from Taylor, thanking me for my time and for giving her the opportunity not only to be better at her job but also to better handle her life. Six months later, we promoted Taylor and gave her more responsibilities. She has been a tremendous gift to our team and to the practice at large. We are all better, thanks to her. Thanks to Dan Sullivan's four Cs, she is more capable and confident than she was. Without the shackles of self-doubt, the sky is the limit for Taylor.

She's not alone; I have found that once people master the four Cs, they can apply them to multiple areas of their lives. Thus, when a new problem emerges, they know they have the strength and tools to work through it. I use this mindset on a daily basis.

I learned later that Taylor had recently received an offer for a position with her previous employer. Although the offer included a bigger title and more money, she turned them down. Why? As we established, it's often not about the money; it's about how you make your teammates feel. Taylor appreciated that we provided her with a clear philosophy that matched her own, and with the opportunity to reach the next level.

Here, I'm going to quote another football great, the Dallas Cowboys' first head coach, Tom Landry, who led the team to victory many times during his twenty-nine-season tenure. He said, **"A coach is someone who tells you what you don't want to hear, who has you see what you don't want to see, so you can be who you have always known you could be[39]."** That's what I was determined to do for Taylor, and what I aim to do for all my staff.

After Taylor's review and her kind letter, I wrote one in return. We also gave her a raise and sent her a gift certificate to a nearby restaurant so she and her boyfriend could enjoy a nice dinner—all to recognize her service and her willingness to take it to the next level, to strive to be great. We did not make Taylor great. We don't have that power. Taylor was already great. Our role was to unlock the greatness that was already present within her through love and compassion.

Recognize Dedication and Achievements Alike

I also try to recognize the team's efforts in small ways. After I arrive at the office, ready to lead, I greet everyone by name—and with a smile. I ask them how they're doing, bring up something they have mentioned from their personal lives—like the recent sale of their house, or a date they went on the previous weekend. And—most important—I thank them for being there. I try to connect with everyone at least once a day. If I don't see them in the morning meeting, before the first patient arrives, I make a point of stopping by their desk or pausing for a moment in the hallway to check in and share my gratitude. That gratitude is genuine.

A lot of my dental colleagues tell me the most stressful part of their job is working with their staff. I have to say, that's the part of my job I enjoy the most. I love my team. I love developing, nurturing, and supporting them. It's that perspective and approach that makes all of our lives—personal and professional—better.

Summary: Building a Team That Works for Everyone

Teams are often the unsung heroes of dental and medical practices. It takes every member—from the front desk staff to the IT team and doctors—to provide an exceptional patient experience. That means, as team leader or organizational Visionary, it's up to you to build and develop a team that will ensure an extraordinary and safe practice.

To cultivate the right environment for the team and beyond, start with a philosophy. This concept should serve as the backbone of your practice and inform every decision you make, including who you hire (for a refresher on hiring, flip back to the previous chapter), how you train, and the way every member of your team treats patients.

Another essential element is the protocol you set for *every* process. Although no two people are exactly the same, having standardized processes keeps your practice clean, efficient, and safe. When it comes to updating and enforcing those protocols, everyone must set their egos aside. For true success, team members cannot cover for each other. They must be able communicate about others' weaknesses and mistakes, so the team can readjust or reinforce protocols for the sake of improvement.

Although you cannot be responsible for every process that occurs in your practice—at least once your operation grows—you must be responsible for its vision and leadership. That requires constant, gentle pressure: moving that saltshaker back to the center of the table day after day.

Note too that running a team is a privilege, and it should feel like one. Take time to feel and express your gratitude and ensure your team knows they're participating in something bigger than themselves, and you'll see the fruits of your labor in the form of an exceptional practice.

How to Cultivate an Excellent Team

- Start with a strong practice philosophy and hire those who align with it personally and professionally.

- Institute a set of protocols that prevent mistakes and empower everyone to fulfill their responsibilities.

- When mistakes occur, review the four questions and develop a new protocol if necessary.
  - What happened?
  - Why did it happen?
  - What can we do so it doesn't happen again?
  - What have we learned from it?

- Treat your team members with respect and reward them for their hard work. They provide a "wow" experience for patients; you should wow them on occasion as well.

- Every team needs a leader and Visionary. Make sure your team knows they can look to you for direction on tasks both big and small.

- Ensure you have an Integrator on board to bring your vision to life.

- Apply constant, gentle pressure to keep everyone on track.

- Don't forget to express your gratitude!

Questions to Consider

- Does every member of your team know—and align with—your philosophy?

- How clear are protocols in your practice? Are they crystal clear?

- Do you have a checklist for every process in your practice?

- Do you have a culture of openness and trust?

- Does everyone have the knowledge and power to do their jobs to the best of their ability?

- Have your teammates been given permission to tell another teammate or yourself if they are making a mistake or if something needs improvement?

- Do all members of your team wear the same uniform? If not, should they?

- Are you acting as a Visionary for your practice and your team? If not, do you have a Visionary for your team?

- Are you providing the leadership and support they need?

- Who are your Integrators?

- How often do you show or tell your team how much you appreciate them?

9

Those Who Can Teach, Do

The Value of Mentorship

I remember the excitement I felt attending my first peri-odontal lecture hosted by the Northeast Society of Periodontology, a prestigious group of periodontists that met regularly in Manhattan. Barely out of my residency program, I registered as early as I could to watch Dr. John Pritchard, a renowned periodontist from Texas, lecture that day. In dental school, I had read his textbooks and learned to use instruments bearing his name. In that moment, I felt a bit starstruck.

He stood at the podium, projecting x-rays he had taken back in the forties on the wall using a slide carousel. He had written the dates on each one in Magic Marker. It wasn't the most elegant or technologically savvy presentation by the standards of the mid-eighties, but I was in awe of him.

He was a mentor of sorts, even though we'd never met—an example of what my career could be.

Some of my peers, other young periodontists in the room, clearly didn't feel the same way. They cracked jokes about the old man on stage and his aging slides. I knew even then, however, that we were witnessing something important. I knew how rare it was for a doctor to have the same passion for his work so many years into his career.

I turned to them and said, "If I'm still alive in my eighties, and I still have that much passion about cases I did forty years earlier, I'll consider myself pretty lucky." The latter part turned out to be true.

Today, at the age of sixty-eight, it brings me tremendous joy to look back at patients I treated in 1985—around the same time I watched John Pritchard at that podium—because those patients still have their teeth.

There's a joke in our profession: If you want to be a successful periodontist, move your office every five years. That way, you never have to see your failures. I've been in the same location for more than thirty-five years. I see my patients immediately after treatment, and I am fortunate enough to see many of them two or three decades later as well. I didn't have nearly as much experience when I first treated them, but thanks to my mentors, I had been trained well.

If a periodontist were to look at those same cases today, they might recommend removing or replacing the patients' teeth with implants. I had been trained before implants were part and parcel of routine dental care, and as such, I had to learn how to save teeth at a time when alternatives were not available. My training included making long-term treatment plans so that what I did then would last not for a handful of months or years but perhaps for the rest of the patient's life.

In the '80s, when I began to practice, I modified what I had learned from Abe Shuster, Colin Richman, Ralph Gray, Gerald Kramer, Myron Nevins, Burt Langer, Dennis Tarnow, Tom Van Dyke, Steven Offenbacher, Jan Lindhe, Per-Ingvar Brånemark, Harold Löe, Arnie Weisgold, Leonard Abrams, Bill Robbins, David Garber, Maurice Salama, Michael Pikos, Craig Misch, Dennis Tarnow, and many others to develop a surgical procedure to treat patients with severe periodontal disease without causing any aesthetic disfigurement.

In fact, in 2018, I published a three-decade follow-up on those patients in the *Compendium of Continuing Education*.[40] For that, I have another mentor to thank: Dr. P. D. Miller, an eighty-four-year-old periodontist who called me one Sunday morning and challenged me to write the article.

Lifelong Lessons from the Father of Periodontal Plastic Surgery

About four months earlier, I had presented on the topic at the International Society of Periodontal Plastic Surgeons, hosted by fellow periodontist Dr. Peter Nordland from La Jolla. In the audience was Dr. P. D. Miller, the father of periodontal plastic surgery. He was one of the first periodontists to discuss the concept of plastic surgery with gingival tissues, and he had been instrumental in my career—teaching me techniques to augment soft tissue around teeth to cover their roots. Dr. Miller was a mentor—not only to me, but to thousands of other dentists and periodontists.

I remembered sitting in a conference room at the Pierre Hotel on Fifth Avenue in Manhattan at another meeting of the Northeast Society of Periodontists, around 1986. I was there for a lunch and learn with Dr. Miller, and I'd had the chance to sit with him. There, at a sold-out table of twelve people over chicken and vegetables, he'd passed around

Polaroids of his work and walked us step by step through the procedure he was describing. To me, he was a god. That hadn't changed much in the intervening three decades.

Over the years, I had gotten to know him quite well, and after I lectured, he came over to tell me I should publish my findings. "Okay, I will," I said, though I had no intention of writing up the article. After all, by then I had been practicing the technique for thirty years—it seemed old hat to me. Soon after, I forgot about the conversation. That is, until my phone rang. I did not know it at the time, but my good friend and colleague Dr. Robert Levine—also a protégé of Dr. Miller—had challenged him to "nail down Sonick".

I first met Bob Levine at a preparation course for the American Academy of Periodontology Specialty boards at LSU in 1986. We bonded over our passion for treating periodontal disease. I found him to be a kindred spirit. Today, I consider him one of my brothers. On a weekly basis, we share ideas, cases, concepts, and our passion for what we do.

We even meet regularly with others as part of what we call our "Secret Study Club." Bob Levine, Bobby Butler, Bob Faiella, Brad McAllister, Jeff Ganeles, Jeff Thomas, and I started the group in 2006 as a way to share knowledge and feedback with likeminded colleagues. We wanted to create what Napoleon Hill refers to as a mastermind group, a term he coined in 1925 in his book *The Law of Success*.[41] The group is still together today and now includes our newer partners Rui Ma, Stephanie Koo, Phil Fava, Fred Norkin, Liliana Aranguren, Thomas Eshraghi, Justin Zalewsky, Alan Farber, Monish Bhola, Mitch Godat, Grant King, Jennifer Doobrow, and David Rosania. It has been invaluable during the COVID-19 pandemic. During the past several months, we have met each week to share our insights on the virus, how it has affected the profession, and ways to practice safely—from personal protective equipment to air purification systems. Thanks to my bond with Bob Levine, and that of the group, we have been able to manage the crisis safely and sanely. Thus, it almost goes without saying that he knew me well enough to send Dr. Miller my way.

I was sitting in my basement on a Sunday reading when I answered Dr. Miller's call. "Mike, how's the article coming?" he asked.

"Well, I haven't gotten around to it," I answered hesitantly. Between working full time in my practice, lecturing, and teaching, writing an article was not at the top of my list of priorities.

In that moment, Dr. Miller did something I often do for my employees, students, and children: he pinned me down and got a date.

"When will you get to it?" he asked.

"I'll have it done in two months," I replied.

"I want you to say it."

"I'll have it done in two months," I repeated.

"That's not what I want you to say." Now, P. D. Miller is from Memphis, Tennessee. Even in his eighties, he stands at six feet one, a proud Southern gentleman who is very kind—and also has the capacity to be very intimidating. "Here's what I want you to say: 'Dr. Miller, I promise and commit to writing this article within two months.'"

"Okay," I said.

"No, I want you to say it."

I did.

And I did what I had agreed to do, too, finishing it in two months and publishing it about six months later. If it weren't for Dr. Miller's mentorship and the challenge he presented me with, I can assure you I wouldn't have gotten around to it—certainly not in two months and probably not ever.

These days, Dr. Miller's eyesight is failing, so he is dictating what he knows into books and putting them online. Recently, he produced an online textbook that he has made available at no charge. He put my article in that textbook, dictating it and summarizing its important points for his readers. I remain in awe of his greatness and his continued generosity. It is said that we stand on the shoulders of giants, and he is certainly one of those giants for me.

Dr. Miller has given me a great gift, not only by mentoring me but by serving as a role model for my own teaching and mentoring aspirations.

To Be a Mentor, You Must First Be Teachable

Over the years, I have grown to understand that **the importance of mentorship cannot be overstated.** Today, I have mentors not just in my career but also in physical fitness, nutrition, the future of technology, entrepreneurial health, leadership, and many other areas. I have come to recognize that I only know so much, and that there is immense value in seeking out others who are experts in their fields.

To be a mentor, you must first be teachable. You have to be open to change.

You may have heard the following joke:

"How many psychiatrists does it take to change a light bulb?"

"None; the light bulb has to want to change."

The same is true for you. You have to be open to the lessons that will come your way. In doing so, you're constantly making yourself vulnerable by letting others in.

It can be hard to put your ego aside and admit that you need help, but we all have so much to learn. The world's data double every two years, which means it is impossible to grasp more than the smallest fraction of knowledge out there. The more you realize just how much you don't know, the better off you are, because you then leave room for learning.

It is easy to be arrogant and think we know what we do not know. Lack of humility serves as a blockage to life experiences and to the wisdom of others. The upshot is that we filter out some really useful information, and we become committed to staying the same, often uninformed. One of my mentors, Peter Diamandis, says, "The day before something is a breakthrough, it's a crazy idea."[42]

The following diagram depicts our relationship to all of the knowledge out there. There's what we know, what we know we don't know, and what we don't know we don't know. You'll notice that what we don't know we don't know constitutes the largest portion, by far.

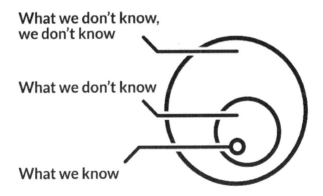

Without a mentor, your personal knowledge limits your effectiveness because what you know is a truly miniscule amount compared with the exponentially increasing information out there in the world today.

I've seen a tremendous technological shift in the three decades I've been referencing. When I was a resident, we would have to go to the library and make photocopies of the articles we wanted to read. We'd each take turns standing in front of the Xerox® machine, our pockets jingling with the change we'd have to feed it.

The Six Ds of Exponential Technologies

Today, everything is online and digitized. Peter Diamandis, an engineer, physician, entrepreneur, and one of my mentors, frequently references the six-step growth cycle of digital technologies, which he refers to as the Six Ds of Exponential Technologies.[43]

The first step is **Digitization**. Once a product or service is digitized, it is subject to the kind of exponential growth the world is experiencing. According to Diamandis, however, that growth is **Deceptive**, because even exponential growth appears slow at first. As the item's growth picks up speed, it becomes **Disruptive** to its industry, transforming the market.

Next, it becomes **Demonetized**, as the technology becomes cheaper or even free. A case in point is the many mobile phone apps that come with little or no cost at all.

Then, the product or service is **Dematerialized**, as any clunky machinery or material becomes pocket-size. Think about your phone, which likely houses video and photography capabilities, a GPS, and more—all of which once required their own respective machines. For example, in dentistry, we don't take impressions anymore. Instead, we take a scan of the patient's mouth and send it directly—and seamlessly—to a 3D printer somewhere in the office.

Finally, it is **Democratized** and made accessible to many, rather than only those who can afford the latest technology.[44]

Just think—Approximately 5.24 billion of the world's 7.6 billion residents have cell phones. Moreover, the power housed in those little devices is more than what President Ronald Reagan had access to as president!

With the process of digitization in mind, Peter Diamandis is a firm believer that if something can be digitized, digitization must be done. Nowhere in medicine is digitization more evident than in dentistry. Following Peter's advice, our team has made sweeping changes to our office. We have spearheaded the adoption of paperless charts and the elimination of paper. All photographs and x-rays, including our cone beam computed tomography, are digitized as well. Impressions are done by using an electronic scanner, making the older clunky, uncomfortable, gag-inducing impressions a thing of the past. Models are no longer poured and sent to the laboratory. They are printed from the computer image in our office 3D printer. Or the images could be sent directly to the laboratory for fabrication of the restoration without even printing a model—all thanks to digitization.

Sometime in the near future, it may be possible to do a significant percentage of our examinations over the internet—with a patient running a small camera around the inside of their mouth from the comfort of their home. It is thanks to Peter Diamandis's insight and mentorship that I can image a bold future.

Diamandis's Six-D cycle also applies to individual development. Our education levels, experiences, and perspectives change over time, much like the process of digitization. My job has certainly evolved over the years. I started off as a dentist who only practiced dentistry. Then, I realized I had to be a businessperson too—I had to go to the bank and borrow money, learn how to run an office, build a team, and grow it. I had to learn how to be an educator. I had to learn how to take on and work with a partner. And, of course, I had to learn how to incorporate rapid technological changes into my practice. To continue to evolve, I've relied on mentors, experts in various areas—individuals who could help me hone my skills.

Become a Mentor Yourself

It's not just about harnessing the opportunity to learn from experts in mentorship roles. To continue to grow and hone your craft, you must become a mentor yourself.

In *Zorba the Greek*, a novel written by Nikos Kazantzakis, many of life's philosophical questions are explored, centering around happiness and living abundantly.

At one point in the book, Zorba finds an old man on his hands and knees planting an almond tree.

Zorba exclaims, "Hey, grandpa, are you really planting an almond tree?"

The old man, as bent as he was, turned 'round and said: "My boy, I act as though I'm never going to die."

The younger Zorba responded, "I act as though I'm going to die at any moment."[45]

In some ways, mentoring allows for both, enabling you to pass on lessons and seed your legacy—to prepare for your inevitable exit from this world and to ensure your insights live on.

I first learned this from Dr. Dennis Tarnow. I had just finished my residency program, which had a mandatory teaching component, so I was used to working with undergraduates. When I went into practice back in 1984, I did not have many patients. As a matter of fact, at first, I had no patients. What I had instead was a lot of free time. I thought I might be able to fill it with teaching.

I went to New York University to see if I could volunteer there. At the time, Dr. Tarnow was the head of the residency program. In his office, I asked whether I could work there one half-day a week. I'm not sure why—I was just starting out, and I wasn't particularly busy.

"We usually require a full day," he said, "but because you just got out of school, I'll let you put in a half day for the next six months." At the time, I didn't know a lot about Dr. Tarnow. He wasn't very much older than me. Since then, he has become one of the most well-known dental educators and implantologists in the world. He went on to serve as chairman of NYU's Department of Periodontics and Implant Dentistry, and one of the school's wings bears his name. Today, he is director of implant education at Columbia University School of Dental Medicine. But what I'd learn, first and foremost, is that he is selfless and bright, that he has a photographic memory, and that he is tremendously passionate about education. Teaching is his *why*.

Not long after I began teaching at NYU, I went to the head of the department of periodontology at the time, a man named Dr. Sigmund Stahl. I told him I wanted to teach a course on practice management. I didn't quite realize how arrogant it was to approach one of the icons in my field as a newly graduated periodontist and ask to teach about something I didn't have much experience in—if any at all. There were many things he could have said to me, but he replied, "If you want to know something about practice management, talk to Dennis Tarnow."

Dr. Tarnow had his own practice in Manhattan, and he began to school me in how to treat patients. Some of his lessons built on what I had learned from Dr. Myron Finkel: send a note on their birthday (a practice that was meaningful then but has become trite in the age of the internet), give them a bottle of champagne at the end of treatment, send flowers when it's appropriate. After some time, I realized Dr. Stahl had been right: I had more to learn before I would be ready to teach that course.

It's important to remember that mentorship comes from experience. A nineteen-year-old can teach you how to use a computer, but that isn't the same as mentoring. On the other hand, someone in their nineties who may not know the ins and outs of their inbox may be an excellent mentor regarding the impact of rapidly evolving technology on our lives.

I dropped the idea of teaching practice management and put in my half days every Thursday for six months, and then I put in full days once a week for six years. Every time I came to campus, I visited Dr. Tarnow. Although I established my own practice with patients and a busy schedule of my own over the years, I saw my time at NYU as a second residency. I sat in on Dr. Tarnow's residency seminars, listening and taking notes, and eventually he let me help run them.

I learned a lot about dentistry from him, but the things he taught me that I truly cherish didn't have much to do with dentistry at all.

First and foremost, he taught me the value of being a good person, of practicing with integrity. One day, I was walking with him through an NYU clinic, examining patients. When he saw something that another dentist had done poorly, he didn't speak disparagingly about them. Instead, he would say that the case must have been challenging, or that the dentist surely did the best they could. "How can I judge?" he told me when I questioned him about it. "I wasn't there." I never forgot that.

He also taught me to keep it simple. "Don't try to do too many things at once, Mike," he said. "Just do one thing well at a time. One miracle at a time." That became his trademark. I realized how important it is not to overwhelm the patient and the process by trying to do too many things at once. The more layers you add to the situation—in dentistry and in life—the more that can go wrong.

Some of Dr. Tarnow's teachings were even more practical. About twenty-five

> **The more layers you add to the situation—in dentistry and in life—the more can go wrong.**

years ago, we were in a West Coast airport. We had just flown in for the annual meeting of the American Academy of Periodontology. Two other periodontal colleagues, Gary Greenstein (one of the most published periodontists in the United States and a renowned educator) and Vincent Iacono (currently Professor and Department Chair of Periodontology at Stony Brook) were there as well. We stood together, waiting at baggage claim for our luggage to appear on the conveyer belt. Dr. Tarnow turned to me. "I never wait for luggage," he said.

"What do you mean?" I asked.

"I just do a carry-on," he said with a shrug, gesturing to the small rolling suitcase by his side.

"How is that possible?" I asked.

"Let me show you," he said, unzipping his bag in the middle of baggage claim. He took everything out, showing me how to pack a suitcase item by item. As I looked at Dr. Tarnow, unpacking his bag in the middle of the busy airport, I was in awe of his passion for teaching. Dennis Tarnow's willingness to teach in any and all situations is emblematic of a true mentor.

Since that fateful day, I never checked my luggage. I insisted that my family should abide by the same rule, much to their dismay—until about ten years ago when we planned a two-week vacation in France. I remained committed to the no-check policy, but my wife refused. "I have to check a bag," she said. "This trip is just too long."

Well, we arrived, but her bag did not. She had to spend a few hundred dollars replacing everything she had brought. When we finally tracked down the now-damaged bag ten days later, her clothes had been destroyed. Since then, she has embraced the carry-on life no matter where in the world we go or for how long. Thank you, Doctor Tarnow!

Mentor to Identify What You Don't Know

In addition to Dr. Tarnow's lessons, teaching at NYU also taught me a lot. I realized the process of lecturing and working with students shined a light on what I didn't know. There was so much I thought I had mastered, until I tried to articulate it to a young dentist. For example, there are two well-known salivary gland ducts in the mouth: Stenson's duct, which comes from the parotid gland, and Wharton's Duct, which comes from the sublingual gland. I could distinguish between them on a multiple-choice test, but when I was examining a patient and explaining the process to a dental student, I had trouble remembering which was which.

I learned firsthand that the old adage "those who can't do, teach" wasn't really true. In fact, it was the opposite. I had to know exactly what I was doing—and talking about—to help my students learn. **Being a teacher made—and continues to make—me a better doctor.**

In 1990, I met Mr. Ken Beacham, who at the time was director of continuing dental education at New York University School of Dentistry. Dr. Paul Fletcher, a partner in private practice with Dennis Tarnow, introduced us because he thought I would be a good teacher for the school's international program.

After we met, Ken offered me the opportunity to teach for one day a month on a topic of his choosing. I then would spend four to six hours lecturing on it.

One day, I headed into NYU, carrying my case of Kodak carousels for the slide projector, ready to lecture on the assigned topic. When I arrived, I realized that I had taught that day's students—a group of French dentists—twice before. They had already seen every slide I'd brought with me.

Ken handed me a piece of chalk and pointed to the blackboard at the front of the room. I had six hours, a piece of chalk, and no prepared material.

I was very nervous and felt as if I were fumbling through most of my time with them. At the end of the day, I stopped by Ken's office. "Don't ever do that to me again," I said.

He smiled. "Why? I did that to you on purpose. You're a good teacher, and I want to make you a better teacher. Today, you got a little bit better."

Ken's background is in business. He holds an MBA from the University of Georgia, and he got his start selling suits out there. When it came to teaching, he always said, "Be a great teacher and try to give them a good product. Don't worry about what it's going to cost. As we always said back in the store, the **quality remains long after the sweetness of low price has been forgotten.** You always want to give value. That's what our patients want, what our students want; it's what everybody wants."

That lesson has always stuck with me. In any relationship I have—as a father, husband, brother, employer, doctor—I aim to provide value.

Thirty years later, Ken is Assistant Dean of the Linhart Continuing Dental Education Program at NYU College of Dentistry—running the largest department of continuing dental education in the world—and we still work together. We have traveled to more than thirty-five countries around the globe, teaching with one another. He has remained one of my mentors in education.

Ken likes to tell me that I'm among the top five educators he's worked with. One time, I responded, "Yeah, but am I *the* top?"

"You know, Mike," he said, "you can never be *the* top. There's only one Dennis Tarnow." I have to agree. Over thirty-five years after our initial meeting, Dennis still remains my mentor.

The more I taught, the more I learned. And as I observed the progress I was making from teaching, I began picking up other teaching jobs at other schools. I started teaching at the University of Bridgeport's Fones School of Dental Hygiene, the first school of dental hygiene in the world; at the University of Connecticut School of Dental Medicine, where I still teach; and in the Yale School of Medicine residency program at Yale New Haven Hospital. In addition to perfecting my craft, I also developed a network of educators who could mentor me too. And thanks to digitization, these educators are not only in New York and New Haven but also around the globe.

Build Your Own Community of Mentors

It wasn't only through teaching that I acquired these mentors. Back in the 1980s, whenever I attended a meeting or a lecture, I made a point of asking those I respected for their contact information and providing them with mine. I'd ask for permission to call them if I ran into a problem. I found that experts—especially those who are educators—are more than generous with their time. I remember asking Dr.

Harold Shavel for some insight after he spoke at an event. He responded that he was rushing to catch a plane but jotted down his phone number on a scrap of paper and invited me to call him at his home anytime. It was an incredibly generous move that I've seen play out time and again. And when someone agreed or offered to talk to me, I always took them up on it.

As a result, although I have about twenty dental colleagues who compose my local network—due to their proximity to me—I also consider hundreds of dentists around the world to be my colleagues. Thanks to technology and digitization, I can collaborate with someone who is twelve thousand miles away, either in real time or on a short delay. My location no longer limits who can be on my team. **If I connect with someone who has value to me and vice versa, we can be on the same team—even if we are not employees of the same organization.** The expansive network I have built has been one of the greatest benefits of mentorship for me. Like Kevin Bacon, I am no more than six degrees of separation from the vast majority of the great minds I may need to access at any point in time.

Today, when I run into a complication, I simply reach out to my network, sending an email with questions and a photograph or x-ray to nine or ten of my colleagues. I find that, within twenty-four hours, 90 percent of them respond—copying everyone else—so that we all have the opportunity to learn from each other.

And because my network extends across areas of expertise, states, and continents, I'm able to refer patients, friends, and family members to doctors and other professionals around the world too. In addition to keeping a list of top restaurants, I also have one of top doctors. And when I connect with an expert in their field, I ask them for the names of other specialists whom they trust. That knowledge helps me grow and better serve my network.

It's been over thirty-five years since Dennis Tarnow and I first met. A few years ago, he came up to me at a meeting. "I'm very proud of you," he said.

I thanked him.

"You're also one of my biggest disappointments," he continued.

I laughed.

"You could have made something of yourself." I knew what he meant. He always thought I should have been even more academic, spending more time at the university, teaching in a formal situation. But I find ways to teach every day.

Today, thanks in large part to Dr. Tarnow's influence, I look at myself not as a dentist, not as a surgeon, not as a businessperson, but as a mentor—and not just to other dentists.

Recently, I had the opportunity to mentor my son, Jason, as he embarked on a new career. He and his wife, Christina, were in the travel business—and very successfully so—for many years. But when COVID-19 hit, all but obliterating the travel industry, they decided to seek another path and follow their true passion: real estate.

The business model they found themselves working in was entirely different from the travel business. Rather than waiting for clients to reach out to them, they had to connect with and develop a network. They built a website, created a brochure, and began taking photos as a means of connecting. And, after a short time, my son reached out to me for some help.

"You seem to have a network from all over the world," he said. "There's nobody you don't or can't know within one or two phone calls—people who can help you get restaurant reservations across the country or connect you with a leading rheumatologist. What can I do to grow my business?"

"Well," I said, "I don't know anything about real estate. I've never sold a house. I don't even know much about crafting a website. But I do know that I've built my business and most of my life on relationships. I did it through mentoring, by seeking out mentors and mentoring others. It's a process that takes a little risk and courage."

"How do I do that?" he asked. "I need a concrete example."

"Get a piece of paper I told him, "and write the days of the week on it. Jot down five names under each day and call them all. Five on Monday, five on Tuesday, and so on."

"What do I talk about?"

"Just reach out. Tell them what you're doing. By the end of one week, you'll have talked to thirty-five people, all of whom know hundreds of other people. It doesn't matter where they are—Miami or California—they can refer you to friends who need your help." He agreed.

A week later, I called him back and asked how it went. "I did two days out of the last five," he told me.

"That's okay," I said, "It takes an average of sixty-six days to make a habit. Just do it next week and I'll check in."

When I called a week later, he was proud to tell me he had made thirty-five phone calls.

"That's a problem," I responded.

"Why?"

"You should have made seventy. If you keep upping the number, eventually you won't be making phone calls anymore. You'll be answering them. Why? Because you'll be one of the few people who reaches out to show they care about other people. Become that person, and people will want to buy from you." Within six months, he listed two homes and sold three houses—not bad for your first foray into real estate. I am very proud of Jason.

I understood his hesitation to make those calls. People are often afraid to reach out to a potential mentor. They think that someone who knows a lot more than them won't want to give that knowledge away. But I've found it's just the opposite. Those who know a lot want to share what they have learned. **They want to help you get where you want to go. That's certainly always been the case for me.**

Those who know a lot want to share what they have learned.

What's Your Unique Ability?

It was another mentor, Dan Sullivan—an entrepreneur and coach based in Toronto, Canada—who cemented this realization. He taught me that mentorship is my Unique Ability.

Unique Ability is a term he coined to refer to the characteristics and values specific to every individual—the things we are skilled at, passionate about, energized by, and always willing to improve on.[46] Through his Unique Ability Discovery Process, working with Julia Waller, I was able to identify my unique passions and skills, one of which is mentorship. After spending a one-on-one day workshop with Julia, we were able to formally craft my Unique Ability: to constantly learn and improve; to relate honestly and generously; and to share ideas, systems, and knowledge with those whom I mentor to educate and motivate them to improve the quality of their lives.

Sullivan always says, "Always make your future brighter than your past." For me, that means constant evolution. That's why, at sixty-eight, retirement isn't on my radar. I may not be picking up a scalpel and suturing patients for the rest of my life, but I do plan to be mentoring and helping others for the long haul. I see my role as a mentor as an extension of my mission statement in life: to improve the quality of life of everyone I come into contact with.

I've learned that the more you give, the more you receive. A lot of lecturers will forbid their attendees from taking photographs of their slides. They feel their material is their livelihood, and that sharing that content will jeopardize that livelihood.

A number of years ago I was attending a commencement speech at a local university. The commencement speaker was Harry Gray, CEO of United Technologies. He shared a story about the value of education. He held a single dollar bill and thrust his hand into the air. He said that if he had all the money in the world and gave away just one dollar, he would no longer have all the money in the world. However, if he had all of the knowledge in the world and gave it all away, he would have lost nothing. He would still have all of the knowledge in the world.

Inspired by Harry Gray, I share all my lecture material online, on my website for free—digitized and demonetized. Does that decision cost me anything? No. I know the material; no one can take that from me. Those who decide to use it will learn from it. That's the reason I teach. Mentorship encourages the growth of future generations and makes the world a better place. I love mentoring, and my purpose is to make those around me better; sharing that information only serves to improve my life. Teaching selflessly benefits everyone.

I would venture to guess that mentorship and generosity will do the same for you.

Summary: Finding—and Being—a Mentor

By now you know that mentorship is essential to advancement, both personally and professionally. To cultivate growth and success, you should look for opportunities to learn from mentors, and to be one yourself.

The first step—especially if you're young or new to a particular skill or career—is to find a mentor. You don't want to be the smartest person in the room. Although it may provide an ego boost, it certainly doesn't foster growth.

How do you find a mentor? Find someone who has what you want. Not everything you want—that person doesn't exist—but some of it, whether it's a skill, a career, or a home life you'd like to have.

We are often hesitant to seek out a mentor because we don't know whom to choose. There is nothing that prevents you from moving on if it's not the right match, or if you outgrow the relationship. It doesn't say anything about the effectiveness of the individual you were working with, or of your experience to date—only that at the current moment in time, it's not the right fit.

For example, I've since modified many of the techniques I learned from some of the greats in dentistry. New technology, tools, insights, and personal experience have allowed me to build on or alter my approach. That's my prerogative. It's part of growing professionally. But it doesn't make their impact on me any less significant. Don't be afraid to experiment. The price of not trying something new is inevitably greater than the failure of not trying anything at all.

Next, look for passion. Look for someone who loves what they do. If someone has truly tapped into their Unique Ability, their job is no longer work. They're in it for the love of the game, not the paycheck.

They also must be willing to share it. If they have a skill you don't, but they're not generous with it, they're not going to be a good mentor. How do you know whether they're willing to share? It's simple: ask. Ask anyone and everyone you admire if you can tap into their knowledge and contact them when you have a problem. If they say yes, don't be shy about reaching out.

How do you become a mentor yourself? Be generous. When someone asks for your input or insight, provide it— readily. If you do not know the answer, be curious. Einstein said that curiosity is more important than knowledge, and I agree. If you do not know the answer, seek out someone who does. Doing so only serves to expand your network.

> How do you become a mentor yourself? Be generous. When someone asks for your input or insight, provide it—readily.

Seek out teaching opportunities. **Sharing what you know makes all of us better.** Some of the richest people in the world—Warren Buffett, Bill Gates—are known not only for their accomplishments but also for how much they give away. They know that doing so enhances—rather than detracts from—their wealth, both materially and emotionally.

The Benefits of Mentorship

- Mentorship makes you a better doctor or professional, enabling you to reap and share knowledge.

- It enables you to develop a network on which to rely if a complication arises.

- Those connections also help to promote you as a thought leader in your field and beyond.

- Giving in the form of mentorship provides just as many gifts—if not more—than receiving does. The irony is that by giving it away you become more knowledgeable.

- Mentoring makes the world a better place, and when you make the world a better place, your world becomes better too.

- Mentoring makes you a better person.

Questions to Consider

As you think about your past, present, and future experience with mentors, consider the following questions:

- Who have been your mentors?

- What benefits and gifts have they bestowed?

- How has working with mentors improved your life?

- Has a lack of mentorship hampered your growth?

- Do you feel you are teachable?

- Have you ever been afraid of asking for help? Why?

- What would you have done differently if you had worked with a mentor? (For example, would you have reached out to a potential mentor you were too scared to contact or left a relationship with a mentor that was no longer serving you?)

- What can you do to better mentor and support others?

- Dan Sullivan states that we do not have to know how to do everything. There is a *who* for every *how*. Are you able to find the *whos* in your life?

- Who are you a *how* for? Whom do you mentor?
- Are you comfortable sharing everything you know?
- Have you built a community of people in your life that you can always count on for providing you with information that you do not possess?
- How large in your network of colleagues?
- Do you find connection with others valuable?

10

Do Your Insides Match Your Outsides?

Building Integrity in Your Practice and Beyond

Whenever I go into a restaurant, the first thing I do is head to the bathroom. If it's not pristine—as thoughtfully curated as the artwork or the table settings—I leave. Mops resting against the wall, a stack of highchairs and booster seats, or a haphazard pile of slightly damp, crinkled paper towels are enough to send me packing. I believe that if the staff is willing to let that space look a mess, just imagine what the kitchen—a place the average customer can't see—must be like!

I used to think the bathroom was the most important room in our office—an indicator of how we care for all of our spaces, including our patients' mouths. But one day, I learned that wasn't the case.

The Most Important Room in the House

William Raveis was referred to our office as a new patient. I knew who he was before I met him. Raveis founded and helmed one of the most successful privately owned real estate brokerages in the United States, William Raveis Real Estate. As a result, he had become a household name in my town. My mother had worked for him as a real estate agent back in the 1980s, too, and I heard about his many successes often.

Raveis was born in Bridgeport, Connecticut, and grew up very poor. As a kid, he worked as a caddy at the local golf club and vowed that he'd eventually build wealth like the rich people whose bags he carried. That fueled his drive to grow a nationally renowned real estate behemoth.

When he finally arrived at my office after canceling a number of appointments, I was happy to see him. But when I went to introduce myself, he was preoccupied, fielding calls from two cell phones, one in each hand.

After a beat, he responded to my greeting. "Hi," he said, "I'm Bill."

"Hi, Bill. I've always wanted to meet you," I told him. "You finally made it to the office. You're busy, huh?"

"Yeah," he replied, distracted again by something on one of his phones.

"How many employees do you have?" I asked him, after another long pause.

"Forty-five hundred" he said, still staring at the screen.

"You've got forty-five hundred employees, and no one can answer the phone for you?" I asked.

He looked at me and smirked. I could guess he was thinking something along the lines of *Who is this cocky jerk?*

"Sorry," I said, "I'm just a little intimidated by you." I told him.

"No, you're not," he said. "But that's okay. I've already checked you out. You're okay with me."

"How do you know?"

"I checked out the most important room in your office," he said.

"Oh, the bathroom?" I responded confidently.

"No, the most important room in any house."

"It's not the bathroom?"

"It's the basement," he said. "Your building is over one hundred years old, and your basement is pristine."

"How do you know what my basement looks like?" I asked. It certainly wasn't on the way to the treatment room we were in.

"When the staff wasn't looking, I ran into the basement. It's pretty impressive."

That wasn't the case when I bought the building. The basement had all sorts of issues, from asbestos to a thick layer of sludgy water and random car parts. I'd invested thousands remediating everything about the building, including the basement, and had spent hour upon hour cleaning the space myself. It really was pristine.

Having broken the ice with our banter and Bill's unusual observation, we went on to have a great relationship. Each year, Bill organizes an annual bike ride and walk charity event to benefit the Damon Runyon Cancer Research Foundation. Our office team participates in the ride to aid in raising the $500,000 Bill's event donates each year. More than that, our interaction highlighted the importance of integrity, of making sure your insides match your outsides.

No one ever sees the basement of my office building (with the exception of Bill, of course), but I was still committed to putting in the time, money, and effort to ensure it was as clean and well-maintained as the rest of my office. **I strive to have my insides—the parts you can't see—match my outsides at work and beyond. That's the hallmark of integrity.**

Michael Koenigs's Advice

Michael Koenigs has helped more than fifty-five thousand people with his marketing services and products and built and sold three businesses. The premise of his argument is this: You can earn a living for *who you are* instead of *what you do*, and that will lead you to true success. Those who have gone on to thrive with his help found ways to make who they are the crux of their work, and it serves as a competitive advantage in every market.

Having met Mike previously at my first Strategic Coach meeting with my mentor Dan Sullivan in Toronto, I ran into him at Peter Diamandis's Abundance360 Community in Beverly Hills. I was always impressed with his generosity; I approached him and asked him what he knew about marketing using artificial intelligence—something I was interested in implementing in my practice.

"I don't know anything about artificial intelligence," he said. "What I do know is that when my insides match my outsides—and my insides are good—people are going to be attracted to me. That's all you've got to know about marketing." **But to reach your full potential, you must become comfortable showing your insides. And by the same token, you must understand the value of working on those insides, even when no one will see them.**

Impeccable Design, Inside and Out

When Steve Jobs designed Apple® computers, he created them as a closed system. He didn't design them to be opened. He still insisted that the insides, those parts no one would ever see, were designed to be just as sleek and beautiful as the computers' outsides.

An Apple engineer once asked Steve, "Why do we have to make the inside so perfect when no one is ever going to see it?"

"I see it, and I know it's there," Steve replied.[47]

When a dentist asks me for advice on how to manage their practice, I make sure to visit their clinic. First, I look at the waiting room. Most of the time, it's in pretty good shape. Next, I check out the bathroom. About 50 percent of the time, things are in order. Even when they're neat and tidy enough, oftentimes the team hasn't taken the time to stock the bathrooms with extra toilet paper and to include amenities such as mouthwash, toothbrushes and toothpaste, rich hand creams, and aromatherapy diffusers that make for a "wow" experience. But the true test is in their dental sterilization area and laboratory, a place the patients never see.

Most of the time, the room itself looks fine on first glance. Until I open up the cabinets. Often, I find a jumbled mess. Occasionally, I see a system that can't make sense to anyone other than the person responsible for that particular area. If everything isn't labeled, alphabetized, and organized in a manner that could be deciphered by anyone, I realize that the staff doesn't care what the practice's insides look like. When that's the case, I ask whether I can see the dentist's private office.

"Why would you want to see that?" they'll inevitably ask. "Nobody's ever back there."

"Just humor me," I respond. What do I find? Stacks of papers on every surface. A private shower filled with boxes of gauze and masks and gowns. Piles of dirty laundry that the dentist intends to take home and wash at the end of the week. That's when it all becomes clear.

If a dentist is having trouble getting their team to follow their lead, run an orderly practice, keep things neat and clean, and stay on top of the workload, it's because their insides don't match their outsides. And as you already know, every aspect of a practice's culture begins at the top. **If you want your practice's insides to match its outsides, *your* insides must match *your* outsides.**

The Toll of Living a Lie

Of course, that's not an easy thing to do. And that's why most of us don't take steps to make sure our insides and outsides match. Worse, that disparity takes a toll on every aspect of our existence. Why? When your insides don't match your outsides, you live a lie. And as a result, you feel like you're less than, like a phony. And those feelings are palpable on the outside too.

Once in dental school, I was walking down the hall with an acquaintance. He asked whether I played sports in high school. "Yeah," I responded, "two years of basketball." In reality, I'd only played for one year. I'd made what I thought was a harmless adjustment to the truth, figuring my companion wouldn't ever be the wiser. But right behind me was Barry Messinger, my roommate at the University of Connecticut School of Dental Medicine and a high school classmate of mine at Roger Ludlowe in Fairfield, Connecticut.

"Mike, you didn't play two years; you only played one year," he said with a smile.

He was just calling me out as a joke, and it had been a very minor lie—we're talking about my freshman and sophomore years of high school here—but I was so embarrassed. The goal had been to make myself seem just a little better than I felt I was. Clearly, lying wasn't worth the risk. And the truth is, it rarely is.

Be Your Word

As a young man, I used to go down to the Jewish Community Center in Bridgeport, Connecticut. It was an old gymnasium. On Sundays, I'd see all these old men in the locker room—men about the age I am now and a handful of years older. They would sit around in the steam room, completely naked except for the towels draped over their laps, as they waited for their massages. There, they would tell tall tales and bold-faced lies. They would talk about the remarkable athletic careers they'd had in their younger days, brag about how much money they had, share stories of the sexy young women who flirted with them at the grocery store, and more. As a young guy, I watched with a sense of amusement—and a tinge of sadness. These men were in their late sixties, seventies, and eighties, and they still felt the need to lie. In fact, I called the chairs they sat in the lying chairs—a little inside joke with myself. *If you're sitting there, you're lying,* I'd think as I walked past.

Today, I see those lies creep up in my own interactions with people my age. Colleagues, friends, and acquaintances of mine are beginning to retire. They want to go to lunch and talk about the past, inflating it as they go. Although the setting may be different, those conversations feel similar: they want to plop down in a chair for a long while, the truth barely concealed as they rewrite the stories of their lives.

Retiring—or the desire to craft a new history for myself—is not on my radar. The desire to do that comes from failing to live in truth or integrity. As my mentor Dan Sullivan asks, "Why would you retire from something you love?"

One of my father's tenets was "be your word." That's how I've tried to live my life. As he explained, it's a whole lot easier than the alternative, because you don't have to remember the lies you tell. It's about more than just telling the truth, though. You must tell it with compassion. **Make sure your truths don't hurt others.**

Many of my patients come in with a terrible infection and bad breath, but delivering that information to them in a matter-of-fact manner would only hurt them. Although it's my duty to tell them the truth about their condition, I must do it with kindness and sensitivity. To do that, I always couple the diagnosis—which may not be good news—with a solution. I never let the problem dangle. Doing so only serves to stoke patients' fear, a technique some use to coerce them into a particular procedure.

> I always couple the diagnosis—which may not be good news—with a solution. I never let the problem dangle.

Don't Feed the Fire of Fear

A colleague once told me that he would often tell patients that their periodontal problems could lead to heart disease, and then he'd wait for their response. He reported that they'd react with a look of panic, and that sometimes they'd even cry right in front of him. And that typically, they'd go home, come back, and tell him they wanted to do the treatment he'd recommended because they didn't want to die of heart disease. It was essentially a sales tactic based on fear.

There are forty-three muscles in the face. You can see fear registering across them, tension collecting on the brow and in the muscles of the jaw. You know when you're stoking fear in someone.

I refuse to use fear as a motivator in my practice. Instead, I work on generating the opposite of fear, which is knowledge. When patients are told the truth and given a solution to their problem, those facial muscles relax rather than tighten. Truth is the antidote to fear. Truth empowers. Most of our fears are based on a false story that we tell ourselves. When a patient comes to see you, you have the opportunity to motivate them through education. **Give them the knowledge to drive the bus of their own treatment—that's what makes for a "wow" experience. Treatment planning is a shared decision-making process between doctor and patient.**

Like Attracts Like

When your insides match your outsides, you attract those with similar values—including your patients and your staff. People often say that opposites attract, but that's not actually true. Like attracts like. Gino Wickman, the founder of the Entrepreneurial Operating System®, discusses the importance of one's insides matching outsides, too. He explains that you must establish your business's core values and that those values must be present in the people you hire—as we discussed in our hiring chapter.

Recently, one of my key employees, Emilia, decided to take a sabbatical. Having been with us for nine years, she was the backbone of our clinical team. At the end of Emilia's last meeting with us, Dr. Stephanie Koo, our newest periodontist, spoke up. "It's Emilia's last day," she said. "Let's go around and say a few things." We went around the room, and people rattled off the traits Emilia embodied. Everything they mentioned was part of our core values: health, integrity, servant-hearted, teamwork, and education.

When it was my turn, I told the story of how I first hired Emilia. Almost ten years earlier, when she'd come in for her interview, Emilia mentioned that she worked for Dr. Jeff Shapiro. Dr. Shapiro and I had worked closely together in the windowless basement of Galleria Mall in White Plains back in 1984, when we were both just starting out. I left to set up shop in Connecticut, and he went on to build one of the most successful practices on Wall Street in Manhattan. I consider Jeff one of my dental soulmates. He is one of the best, if not the best, dentist in Manhattan. It is not only his clinical skill that makes him special. What separates him is his integrity. He and his practice embody the principles of a patient-centered practice. I knew that I could count on him for an honest employee reference.

I called Dr. Shapiro and told him I was thinking of hiring her. "Is she any good?" I asked.

"No, she's not," he said.

I asked, "What do you mean?"

"She's not good; she's great. As a matter of fact, she's the best dental assistant I've ever had. You'll be lucky if she works for you," he finished. And he was right.

By the end of my story, all nine of my dental assistants were crying because Emilia had made such an impact on them. Some had been there for as long as Emilia had. Others had been with us less than a year—and they were crying the hardest because she had made such a difference for them so quickly.

Emilia's insides match her outsides, and those of our practice. And that has enabled her to give everyone she's encountered such a fantastic experience. Her integrity—and the principles that make her who she is—show through in every situation. To run a strong practice, as well as to have a great life, those principles must be present.

Staying Principled, Even When the Going Gets Tough

When you practice principle-centered dentistry or medicine—anything, really—you have to be prepared for a harsh reality: not everyone is going to like you or what you do.

During my partner Dr. John's first year in practice, he took great pains to make sure no one was upset with him. One day, I pulled him aside. "It's not possible to be a great doctor and have nobody upset with you," I said. **"You have to make a decision right now: do you want to practice with integrity, or do you want to be liked by everyone? You can't have both. It's just not going to happen. When you practice with integrity, though, you will be respected."**

What does integrity mean in the realm of dentistry and medicine, exactly? It means you must stop being procedure-oriented, and start being preventative. It means looking at the person in front of you as a person rather than a task or a procedure you must handle or complete. It means being honest with them about what is in their best interest. It means allowing them to drive the bus, to take control over their care after you provide the education piece and let the chips fall where they may—even if doing so seems like it will create a challenging financial situation for you.

As a periodontal resident at Emory University, I inherited patients from the residents who came before me and had graduated. One of my predecessors was a charming, good-looking guy from South Carolina. He was a tough act to follow. His patients loved him, so much so that, after he completed his residency, he opened a private practice fifteen miles away, and some patients followed him there, even though his services cost significantly more money than the ones they had been receiving at Emory.

One day, a patient who had followed him when he left returned to the clinic. "What are you doing here?" I asked, telling her I thought she'd stayed with the doctor she liked so much. She confirmed that she had indeed gone to see the other doctor, and now she would be back under our care. "Why?" I asked, confused.

"Well, when I went to see him at his private practice, he looked at me differently. He looked at me with *cash register eyes.*" The moment she said it, my mind conjured an image of the handsome doctor with dollar signs where his pupils would be.

Now, we all have bills to pay, and those fresh out of dental school often face a tremendous debt burden: today, it's around $292,159 on average, according to the American Dental Education Association.[48] The opportunity to make more money is one of the primary incentives of setting out on your own. If that becomes your primary goal, however, your true motives will show through. In short, doing work only for the money undermines your integrity, and integrity is crucial to your work and the positive connections you work so hard to build with your patients.

My first year in practice, I had a patient whom I'll call Johan. Initially, he had nonsurgical treatment: scaling and root planing to eliminate infection and inflammation. As is customary, he returned a month later for his reevaluation examination. At the time, the best practice was to check to see whether deep pocketing remained, and if the pockets were more than 6 mm, gum surgery was indicated.

When I examined him a second time, I saw that Johan still had deep pocketing. "Do I need surgical treatment?" he asked when I explained the situation.

"Yes," I replied, "you do."

"My insurance won't cover anything else this year. Can I wait until next year?" he asked.

It was my first year in practice. I was barely making an income. The money from the procedure would be quite helpful when it came to my own bottom line. I knew, however, that the condition wasn't life-threatening, and we could maintain his health with nonsurgical care until his insurance would cover the cost of the procedure the following year.

"If you tell me I have to do it now, I'll pay for it out of pocket. If it can wait, I'd prefer to do so when my insurance kicks in," Johan said.

I hesitated for a moment, thinking all that through. Finally, my mind flashed to the image of the resident looking at his patient with cash register eyes.

"You can wait until next year," I said.

Johan was forty-two years old when he asked me that question. He died of a massive heart attack three months later. He didn't need the surgery because he was going to be dead in three months. He could have died while I was treating him.

I call that my "Johan moment." It was the moment I chose integrity.

Sometimes, it takes courage to have integrity. I knew that if I told him he didn't have to have the surgery right away, I wouldn't make much-needed money on that patient, in the face of looming expenses. But after the fact, when his wife, who was also a patient of mine, came back to see me, I could look her in the eyes knowing that I had always treated him fairly.

I don't talk much about Johan, but I think about him every day.

I want my patients to know what *they* can do so they can make the right decision for themselves. **It's not my responsibility to get every patient I see to commit to ideal treatment, because what I see as ideal treatment might not be ideal for them. It is my responsibility to educate every patient so they can make the best decision for themselves.**

Information Is the Antidote to Buyer's Remorse

To practice with integrity, before you begin treatment, you must inform every patient of the cost, risks, and benefits of each treatment option. If you don't, chances are they will have buyer's remorse. Patients tell me all the time about what they wish they had known about before going through a particular procedure:

I thought that once I had a tooth crowned, I would never get decay.

I didn't realize that if I'd had the bypass surgery, I wouldn't have heart disease today.

You mean root canals can fail?

I see the dentist twice a year; how can I have gum disease?

I have a bridge. Do you mean I could have had an implant instead and not had to cut down the adjacent teeth?

When questions like the latter two arise, I explain that I can't guarantee what I do will last for life. No doctor can make that guarantee. If an unforeseen issue arises, however, I will address it without an additional charge. When I provide all of that information—about everything that could happen, good or bad, and how I'll deal with whatever comes up,

I enable them to make the decision that's best for them and go into it with their eyes wide open.

Many times, it's not just about addressing what I believe is the right way to go; it's about saving the patient from themselves. Often, patients will tell me what they want. Very frequently, what they want is not the right course of action from a medical perspective. Here too, integrity comes into play.

When I'm not sure about the right course of action, or when the path I believe to be the right one falls outside my area of expertise or regular practice, I don't hesitate to refer patients to someone else. When patients come to me with facial pain, I send them to Dr. Brijesh Chandwani, a TMJ expert. When they have impacted third molars, I send them to an excellent surgeon who deals with that all day long. I refer out for root canals to Dr. Joe Zerella, a local endodontist, because he does twenty a day, whereas I did my last one in 1984.

When patients ask me to handle these procedures myself because we have an existing relationship and they like and trust me, I still refer them out. I tell them that liking me has nothing to do with the quality of care they'll receive or my ability to provide excellent treatment. Part of what makes me good at what I do is my willingness to tell patients what I'm not good at. That requires real honesty and a lack of ego.

Note, too, that sometimes practicing with integrity is about advising patients as to what they *don't* need. Dentists often refer patients to a periodontist because they have gum recession. The periodontist may automatically choose to do a gum graft because that is what the patient and referring dentist expect. Most people who come to me for gum grafts, however, don't actually need one. I perform the procedure on only about 30 percent of the patients who come in for that purpose. I have rarely seen a patient lose a tooth because of gum recession.

When you practice with integrity, you may find that you spend less of your time doing what you're trained to do. I spend much of my day counseling people on what they need and putting those who received the wrong treatment back together. The average patient comes to my office having had a lot of dentistry during the course of their life. Still, their mouth is in a bad state because their dentist, or dentists, didn't take them through comprehensive treatment planning, most of the dentistry hasn't been performed ideally, and the patient hasn't done their part—most likely because they were never told what their part was. Before treatment all patients are informed of their responsibility, if they wish to maintain their health. They must commit to a lifelong comprehensive maintenance program. This is clearly stated at their first visit, although in reality, only 15 percent of our patients follow our instructions. Honest communication is the cornerstone of all great treatment, and that takes integrity.

It's All about the Basics

Establishing and maintaining integrity is all about the basics:

- Always tell the truth.
- Motivate with knowledge, not fear.
- Practice servant leadership.
- Teach others what you know without expecting any- thing in return.
- Get eight hours of sleep.
- Exercise daily.

- Practice mindfulness.
- Eat healthy foods.
- Drink plenty of water.
- Stay fit.
- Continue to educate yourself.
- Be nice to everybody.
- Do your best.

You must constantly return to the basics. It's that constant, gentle pressure that Danny Meyer talks about—always moving the saltshaker back to the center of the table. That's the secret to building a practice and living with integrity. Focusing on the basics will get you farther, personally and professionally, than anything else when it comes to cultivating success.

Summary: Living and Working with Integrity

Integrity goes beyond what people can see. It means maintaining every area of your practice and life with the same moral compass and attention to detail simply because it's the right thing to do.

Remember, the most important parts of your office aren't the ones that patients see. The private spaces, such as cabinets, the basement, and your office, matter just as much as your waiting and treatment rooms and, of course, the bathroom. Your insides—the parts others can't see—should match your outsides. That's the hallmark of integrity.

When your insides match your outsides, it's because your values drive you. When that is true, you readily exhibit your values to the world, and you will draw people—patients, team members, mentors, and friends—to you.

In the same way, as you commit to practicing with integrity, even when you know no one will see what you've done, you will set the tone for your entire team. They will model the integrity you embody—or lack thereof.

Meanwhile, when your insides don't match your outsides, you live a lie. You feel like a phony. And those feelings are palpable on the outside.

To practice with integrity, you must tell the truth with compassion. Don't use fear as a means of motivating patients to follow your recommendations. Instead, provide them with the education to make an informed decision, and then follow their lead. That's how you do good work.

Questions to Consider

- Do your insides match your outsides, or is your judgment occasionally colored by wanting people to like you, your bottom line, or another factor?

- Do you see your values represented in those of your team?

- Is every crevice of your office pristine—even the areas patients don't see?

- Do you have a consistent, well-crafted message? To your patients? To your team?

- Do you have clearly defined treatment goals?

- When it comes to explaining a particular course of treatment, are you focused on educating patients or on influencing them to follow your recommendation?

- Do you trust your well-informed patients to make the right decisions for themselves?

- What matters more to you: that people respect you or that they like you? Is it possible to have both?

- Telling patients what they need often requires a tolerance of conflict. Are you comfortable telling patients, teammates, or colleagues' uncomfortable truths?

- Do you find it difficult to inform patients of their current dental or health status?

- Do you believe that you could build a niche practice based on integrity?

Note to Reader

I hope you have enjoyed reading this book and accompanying me on my journey. Developing a philosophy of care takes time, patience, and practice. Perfecting it is not easy. Don't be discouraged. The lessons presented here have taken me years to learn, and I am still learning. That is the beauty of this life. It excites me that there is always another challenge, another opportunity, another hill to climb.

People are fascinating and working with them is a privilege. I am always intrigued by the unique differences in the people I meet, whether they are patients, friends, colleagues, or other service providers. I feel blessed to have been given the opportunity to have patients entrust me with their care.

I am often invited to speak to groups of people and organizations. I am pleasantly surprised that the message conveyed in **Treating People Not Patients** resonates with not only healthcare providers and people in the hospitality business but anyone whose focus is on other people. Namely, almost everyone.

Learning without mentorship puts you at a disadvantage. I would like to offer you the opportunity to receive additional training. Teaching and helping others is my passion, and nothing would excite me more if I could assist you on your journey to provide over-the-top, excellent patient and customer care. For further training, I encourage you to check out our website www.peoplenotpatients.org.

Appendix: The Little Things

Business, like life, is all about how you make people feel.
It's that simple, and it's that hard.

—Danny Meyer, Founder of Shake Shack
and Author of *Setting the Table*

The success of any business is dependent on thousands of little things that are done daily by all team members to make the patient or customer experience great. All of us have had customer service experiences that were overwhelming and made us feel great. We rush back to those businesses. Making the patient experience great is the sine qua non of a successful practice. Below is a list of "the little things" that our team has compiled.

Be nice to people.

- Treat patients with integrity.
- Be available.

- Be honest.
- Practice patience—all the time.
- Follow biological principles.
- Do not rush—take your time.
- Be on time.
- Smile.
- Create a friendly atmosphere in the office.
- Make sure your team is full of friendly and genuine personalities.
- Treat team members as well as you treat patients.
- Inform before you perform.
- Compliment everyone freely.
- Respect the patient's needs.
- See the patient as a person, *not* as a procedure.
- Greet patients by name and use their name often.
- Make every patient feel special.
- Be genuinely interested in your patients' well-being—be curious.
- Welcome patients as if they are guests in your home.
- Create a "wow" experience for everyone.
- Play pleasant music in the office—classical, soft jazz.
- Acknowledge when things go right.
- Correct things when they are wrong.
- Keep tissue boxes in every room.
- Offer evening and early morning hours.
- Run on time.

- Inform patients if appointments are running late and apologize.
- Work to ensure your team is honestly happy.
- Remember that money is not what moves "the spirit" of the office, it's people.
- Strive to improve each day.

Create a nice atmosphere by offering the following amenities for guests.

- fresh fruit in the reception area
- coffee, tea, juice, soft drinks, and water
- Sugar in the Raw®, honey, stevia, Equal®, Splenda®, Sweet'n Low®
- milk, cream, or soy milk
- Bose® headphones for all patients, with their choice of music during care
- aromatherapy
- soft, relaxing music playing in all rooms
- warm facial towels with a choice of scents
- interesting books and magazines throughout the office
- fun books and magazines for children in the reception area
- a kaleidoscope in the reception area
- tasteful artwork and ceiling mobiles
- beautiful rose gardens at entranceway
- decorative planters changed seasonally framing doorway
- in-office catering

- in-office lab to make emergency provisions if needed
- umbrellas with office logo at the doorway
- complimentary car service in inclement weather
- uniform and clean appearance of all staff members—including white sneakers

Offer a variety of new, topical magazines.

- *People*
- *Newsweek*
- *Reader's Digest*
- *Architectural Digest*
- *Sports Illustrated*
- *Tennis*
- *Golf*
- *Parents*
- *Rolling Stone*
- *Vogue*
- *Cosmopolitan*
- *Vanity Fair*
- *Men's Health*
- *Connecticut*
- *New York Magazine*
- *National Geographic*
- *Condé Nast Traveler*
- Local or regional travel magazines

Provide interesting books in the reception to reflect our philosophy and promote health.

- *The 7 Habits of Highly Effective People*[49]—Steven Covey
- *The Power of Now*[50]—Eckhart Tolle
- *Younger Next Year*[51]—Crowley and Lodge
- *The Seven Spiritual Laws of Success*[52]—Deepak Chopra
- *Setting the Table*[53]—Danny Meyer
- *Beat the Heart Attack Gene*[54]—Bale and Doneen
- *Don't Sweat the Small Stuff*[55]—Richard Carlson
- *The Little Things*[56]—Andy Andrews
- *Eat, Drink, and Be Healthy*[57]—Walter Willett
- *The Addictocarb Diet*[58]—Bruce Roseman

Hold to the motto that cleanliness is next to godliness.

- Have a dishwasher onsite.
- Make a policy that all staff members pick up trash, lint, and any debris.
- Straighten the magazines many times throughout the day.
- Clean or replace dirty ceiling tiles.
- Redecorate every three to five years.
- Dust and straighten pictures regularly.
- Keep your office and all rooms spotless.
- Pay attention to all corners of your office.
- Replace light bulbs immediately when they go out.

- Keep the grounds meticulously appointed.
- Install new carpeting every two years.
- Paint all in-office trim yearly.
- Wax and polish office floors semi-annually.
- Hire a full-office cleaning service nightly.
- Have the windows cleaned inside and out twice a year.

Have a meticulously clean and well-appointed bathroom.

- toothbrushes and toothpaste
- quality soaps and moisturizers in all bathrooms
- tissue boxes
- toilet seat covers
- aromatherapy
- electric heat at the touch of a finger

Keep your team connected and informed.

- Hold a fifteen-minute daily staff meeting.
- Have a monthly office team meeting with a meal prepared by a teammate.
- Have quarterly team-building days.
- Host a Christmas party for staff and their significant others.
- Offer a team day with over-the-top food and entertainment to celebrate your staff.
- Teach NLP—neurolinguistics programming.

- Profile all team members in one or more of the following personality models:
  - o CliftonStrengths
  - o Kolbe A Index
  - o Culture Index
  - o PRINT® Survey
- Make sure every employee functions in their Unique Ability.
- Offer continuing education opportunities for all team members with meals and salary included.
- Update your online protocol manual weekly.
- Offer yoga to all team members.

Practice silent communication amongst staff.

- lights
- flags
- radios with earpieces
- instant message on computers
- email

Practice professional telephone etiquette.

- Answer your telephone pleasantly.
- Be present with each patient.
- Ask permission to place someone on hold and wait for the answer.

- Never put patients on hold for more than thirty seconds.
- Always answer your phone during the day. Do not close phone service for lunch.
- Have pleasant music on hold.
- Avoid playing infomercials.
- Have an answering service for after hours.

Ensure excellent patient communication, in-office marketing, and reviews.

- Collect preferred methods of communication: text, email, phone.
- Make it simple for patients to schedule appointments.
- Use a communication service such as Demandforce® or Weave.
- Collect patient reviews using applications like Birdeye® (birdeye.com).
- Monitor patients' birthdays, and if a birthday falls within a week of a visit, make sure the entire team is aware to offer well wishes.
- Maintain a constant presence in social media using Facebook, Instagram, and Twitter office accounts.
- Highlight a patient of the month on Facebook.
- Take and display before and after photographs of patients.
- Ask for patient testimonials and display them in the office and online.

- Post articles by or about the doctor on the office website, in the reception area, and on social media.
- Include patient video testimonials on website and social media.
- Display impressive credentials of doctor in the reception area.
- Post photographs of doctor and team members doing charitable work in the reception area.
- Participate as a team in local charities, and let the community know.
- Put a get-to-know-the-team binder in the reception area, on the website, and on social media.
- Be aware when your patients are recognized in media and congratulate them.
- Ask for referrals and use them.
- Send a personal thank-you note to everyone who makes a referral.
- Send condolence, thank-you, and congratulatory cards.
- Reward patient videos and testimonials with gift cards or Sonicare toothbrushes.
- Employ an in-house photographer, IT-support, and marketing person.
- Keep current and tidy brochures of all treatments offered.
- Use a large screen to display treatment options.

Establish policies for scheduling, onboarding new patients, insurance, and payment.

- Get emergency patients in the same day.

- Schedule new patients within one week.

- Allow patients to complete medical history at home or online and email to office before first appointment.

- Request and receive previous radiographs before appointment.

- Send all patients a welcome letter, including medical history, directions, and your mission statement before their first appointment.

- Inform patients of what they can anticipate.

- Thank patients for coming in.

- Be aware of and acknowledge how far a patient travels to see you.

- Allow an hour for new patient consultations.

- File dental and medical insurance as a courtesy.

- Help patients with their dental insurance; they're more confused than you are.

- Give informed consent always.

- Have a written financial policy.

- Offer dental financing, such as CareCredit®.

- Give patients a copy of their financial agreement in advance.

Be intentional about patient education.

- Mail a letter after every new patient examination that includes a treatment plan and timeline. Copy other doctors involved.
- Mail a final letter with thank-you to all patients.
- Hold a post-treatment conference.
- Let patients know of their dental success.
- Offer patients the option to seek a second opinion.
- Use a cost, risk, benefits table. Patients will select the right treatment.
- Show patients their intra-oral photos during their consultation.
- Use your website to educate patients about ongoing, preventative, and essential care.
- Inform patients of your continuing education.
- Perform full examination on *all* patients.
- Offer multiple treatment options.
- Allow patients to make the final decision.
- Offer and encourage spousal consultations.
- Have a mirror on your dental light.

Before treatment, make sure your patient is comfortable and informed.

- Give written preoperative instructions.
- Advise surgical patients to premedicate with pain management aids.

- Before treatment begins, offer clean, dark protective eyewear to patients or a spa mask as an alternative.
- Offer a choice of music with headphones.
- Offer local anesthesia for all procedures, including root planning.
- Offer free nitrous during treatment.
- Perform sterile surgery for implant placements and express this to patients.
- Give adequate written and oral postoperative instructions.
- Call in prescriptions to pharmacy, in advance if possible.

After dental treatment, continue the care.

- Give patients a pain reliever at the end of surgeries or long procedures.
- Use, dispense, and recommend arnica.
- Schedule follow-up or hygiene appointments in advance.
- Offer fruit juices after long procedures.
- Walk or wheel surgical and sedated patients to their car following care.
- Admin and clinical team say goodbye to patients together so they feel extra cared for.
- Call patients the night of any surgery or long procedures. Assistants and doctors should both call, but on different days.
- Call patients again a day or two after the procedures.

Encourage regular visits and good patient hygiene between visits.

- Commit to providing pain-free hygiene appointments:
  - o Train all hygienists to give local anesthetic.
  - o Offer Oraqix® and topical analgesics.
  - o Make nitrous oxide available in all hygiene rooms.
  - o Offer personalized audio analgesia.
- Offer free oral hygiene aids to every patient on every visit.
- Give each patient his or her plaque score percentage at each hygiene visit.
- Give written oral hygiene instructions.
- Follow up regularly with patients.
- Schedule a three-month re-care appointment after any procedure.
- Use a "motivator" to encourage patients to keep hygiene appointments on schedule: "I can tell you are having a hard time cleaning #30. We are going to want to check and clean that again at your next visit."

Maintain a robust referral network with other healthcare and wellness practitioners.

- Become a patient advocate.
- When referring patients to other practitioners, offer to call and schedule their appointment and to send their records immediately.
- Make patient records readily available to other doctors as needed.

- Offer in-office continuing education to patients, dentists, hygienists, and the public.

- Develop strong, trusting relationships with physicians and specialists in *all* specialties and disciplines.

- If your patient is moving away, provide a referral to a dentist in their area. Send a referral letter to the health-care provider and copy the patient.

- Refer patients for specialty care when needed.
  - Other dental specialists
    - Endodontists
    - Periodontists
    - Oral surgeons
    - Orthodontists
    - Oral pathologists
    - TMJ / facial pain authorities
    - Dental anesthesiologists
    - Oral radiologists
  - Internists
  - Otolaryngologists
  - OB/GYNs
  - Cardiologists
  - Plastic surgeons
  - Dermatologists
  - Orthopedic surgeons
  - Psychiatrists
  - Holistic specialists

- o Sports medicine specialists
- o Masseuses
- o Nutritionists
- o Chiropractors
- o Acupuncturists
- o Yoga therapists
- o Healers
- Be holistic—have an open mind.
- Remember we do not heal; the body does.

Here are a few questions to ask your patients to ensure "little things" don't get missed in their care:

- Is there anything that isn't clear to you about what we've discussed?
- What do you dislike about your mouth?
- What do you want to improve?
- Do you grind your teeth?
- Do you have muscle soreness in your face or neck?
- Would you like whiter teeth?
- Do you have a bad taste in your mouth?
- Do you want to get the infection under control?
- Would you like your bone restored?
- Would you like to be able to chew better?
- Would you like to stop bone loss?
- Would you like to stop extensive, expensive dentistry?

- How would like for your mouth to be different?
- How can we help you?
- What do you not like about your smile?
- If we could wave a magic wand, what would you like to see happen to your mouth, your oral and systemic health, your smile?
- For the potential implant patient, emphasize the following:
  - o Implants preserve bone.
  - o Implants never decay.
  - o Implants never need root canal treatment.
  - o Implants preserve natural teeth.
  - o Implants can improve psychological health—make one whole again.
  - o Implants stabilize the prosthesis.
  - o Implants improve masticatory efficiency.

Endnotes

1. Danny Meyer, *Setting the Table: The Transforming Power of Hospitality in Business* (New York, NY: HarperCollins Publishers, 2006).
2. Tait D. Shanafelt et al., "Changes in Burnout and Satisfaction with Work-Life Balance in Physicians and the General US Working Population between 2011 and 2014," *Mayo Clinic Proceedings* 90, no. 12 (December 2015): 1600-13, https://www.mayoclinicproceedings.org/action/showCitFormats?pii=S0025-6196%2815%2900716-8&doi=10.1016%2Fj.mayocp.2015.08.023.
3. Michael Sonick and Debby Hwang, eds., *Implant Site Development* (Hoboken, NJ: Wiley Blackwell, 2012).
4. Harald Löe, Else Theilade, and S. Börglum Jensen, "Experimental Gingivitis in Man," *Journal of Periodontal Research*, 1965 May-June; 36:177-87. DOI: 10.1902/jop.1965.36.3.177
5. Henry Thomas Buckle, "Great Minds Discuss Ideas; Average Minds Discuss Events; Small Minds Discuss People," Quote Investigator, https://quoteinvestigator.com/2014/11/18/great-minds/#:~:text=Buckle%20said%2C%20in%20his%20dogmatic,preference%20for%20the%20discussion%20of

6. Colman Andrews, "These Are the 50 Highest Grossing Restaurants in the US," *USA Today*, August 9, 2018.

7. Meyer. *Setting the Table.*

8. Meyer, *Setting the Table.*

9. Simon Sinek, "Everyone Has a Why. Do You Know Yours?" SimonSinek.com, https://simonsinek.com/find-your-why.

10. Andrew Ibbotson, "Patients Trust Online Reviews as Much as Doctor Recommendations," *Health IT Outcomes*, November 9, 2018, https://www.healthitoutcomes.com/doc/patients-trust-online-reviews-as-much-as-doctor-recommendations-0001#:~:text=Further%2C%20six%20of%20ten%20(59.9,doctors%20based%20on%20negative%20reviews.

11. Malcolm Gladwell, *Blink: The Power of Thinking Without Thinking* (New York, NY: Little, Brown and Co., 2005).

12. Stephen R. Covey, *The 7 Habits of Highly Effective People: Restoring the Character Ethic* (New York, NY: Free Press, 2004).

13. Sonick and Hwang, *Implant Site Development.*

14. Eva M. Krockow, "How Many Decisions Do We Make Each Day?" *Psychology Today*, September 27, 2018, https://www.psychologytoday.com/us/blog/stretching-theory/201809/how-many-decisions-do-we-make-each-day.

15. Milton Glicksman, *AAP News*, October 1996.

16. Suzanne C. Segerstrom and Gregory E. Miller, "Psychological Stress and the Human Immune System: A Meta-Analytic Study of 30 Years of Inquiry," *Psychol Bull*, 2004 Jul; 130(4): 601–30.

17. Alex Blumberg and Adam Davidson, "Accidents of History Created U.S. Health System," *NPR*, October 22, 2009. https://www.npr.org/templates/story/story.php?storyId=114045132.

18. Blumberg and Davidson, "Accidents."

19. Blumberg and Davidson, "Accidents."

20. "History," CMS.gov, https://www.cms.gov/About-CMS/Agency-Information/History.

21. "Diagnosis Related Group (DRG)," HMSA.com, https://hmsa.com/portal/provider/zav_pel.fh.DIA.650.htm.

22. "History of Oral health: Dental Insurance," Delta Dental, https://www.deltadental.com/grinmag/us/en/ddins/2018/winter/history-of-dental-insurance.html; "Multitrack Dental Benefits Industry History." NADP Dental Plans. https://www.nadp.org/resources/public/dentalhistory.

23. Ryan Nunn, Jana Parsons, and Jay Shambaugh, "A Dozen Facts About the Economics of the US Health Care System," *Brookings*, March 10, 2020, https://www.brookings.edu/research/a-dozen-facts-about-the-economics-of-the-u-s-health-care-system;

24. "Education," Health Policy Institute: American Dental Association, https://www.ada.org/en/science-research/health-policy-institute/dental-statistics/education; "Total Number of Medical School Graduates," KFF.org, https://www.kff.org/other/state-indicator/total-medical-school-graduates/?currentTimeframe=0&sortModel=%7B%22colId%22:%22Location%22,%22sort%22:%22asc%22%7D; "Number of Law Graduates in the United States from 2013 to 2018," Statista.com, https://www.statista.com/statistics/428985/number-of-law-graduates-us.

25. Harrison Cook, "Among 11 Countries, U.S. Ranks last for Health Outcomes, Equity, and Quality," Becker's Hospital Review, July 10, 2019. https://www.beckershospitalreview.com/quality/among-11-countries-us-ranks-last-for-health-outcomes-equity-and-quality.html.

26. Bradley Bale and Amy Doneen, *Beat the Heart Attack Gene: The Revolutionary Plan to Prevent Heart Disease, Stroke, and Diabetes* (Nashville, TN: Wiley, 2014).

27. Atul Gawande, *Being Mortal: Illness, Medicine, and What Matters in the End* (New York, NY: Metropolitan Books, 2014).

28. Renee Deveney, "What Is the Jellinek Curve," The Recovery Village, November 3, 2020. https://www.therecoveryvillage.com/drug-addiction/faq/what-is-jelinek-curve.

29. Charles Revson, "In the factory we make cosmetics; in the store we sell hope," https://www.brainyquote.com/authors/charles-revson-quotes.

30. Robert F. Barkley, *Successful Preventive Dental Practices* (BookSurge Publishing, 2010).

31. Chris Crowley and Henry S. Lodge, MD, *Younger Next Year: A Guide to Living Like 50 Until You're 80 and Beyond* (New York,NY: Workman Publishing, 2004).

32. Bill Taylor, "Why Zappos Pays New Employees to Quit—And You Should Too," *Harvard Business Review*, May 19, 2008. https://hbr.org/2008/05/why-zappos-pays-new-employees.

33. Taylor, "Zappos."

34. Atul Gawande. *The Checklist Manifesto: How to Get Things Right* (New York, NY: Metropolitan Books, 2009).

35. Danny Meyer, "The Saltshaker Theory," *Inc.*, October 2006.

36. Meyer, "The Saltshaker Theory."

37. Gino Wickman and Mark C. Winters, *Rocket Fuel: The One Essential Combination That Will Get You More of What You Want from Your Business* (Dallas, TX: BenBella Books, Inc, 2015).

38. Adam Brownlee, "McDonald's Corporation—A Real Estate Empire Financed by French Fries," *Motley Fool*, September 21, 2018, https://www.fool.com/investing/general/2016/03/06/mcdonalds-corporation-a-real-estate-empire-finance.aspx

39. Tom Landry, Goodreads, https://www.goodreads.com/quotes/58284-a-coach-is-someone-who-tells-you-what-you-don-t.

40. Michael Sonick, Rui Ma, and Debby Hwang, "Papillary Retention Flap Design for Pocket Reduction/Regeneration: Case Series with Long-Term Follow-Up," *Compendium*, September 2018.

41. Napoleon Hill, *The Law of Success* (Meriden, CT: Ralston University Press, 1928).

42. Peter Diamandis, Brainy Quotes, https://www.brainyquote. com/quotes/peter_diamandis_690503.

43. Vanessa Bates Ramirez, "Digitized to Democratized: These Are the 6 Ds of Exponential Technologies," *SingularityHub*, December 29, 2017, https://singularityhub. com/2017/12/29/what-are-the-6-ds-of-exponential-organizations.

43. Ramirez, "Digitized to Democratized."

45. Nikos Kazantzakis, *Zorba the Greek* (New York: Simon and Schuster, 1969).

46. "What Is Unique Ability." *Strategic Coach*. https:// resources.strategiccoach.com/themultiplier-mindset-blog/ what-is-unique-ability.

47. Walter Isaacson, *Steve Jobs* (New York: Simon and Schuster, 2011).

48. Kimber Solana, "Erasing Dental Debt: From $200K to Zero in Less Than Three Years," American Dental Association, March 2, 2020, https://www.ada.org/ publications/new-dentist-news/2020/march/from-200k-to-zero-in-less-than-three-years

49. Covey, *The 7 Habits of Highly Effective People.*

50. Eckhart Tolle, *The Power of Now: A Guide to Spiritual Enlightenment* (Novato, CA: New World Library, 2010).

51. Crowley and Lodge, *Younger.*

52. Deepak Chopra. *Seven Spiritual Laws of Success: A Practical Guide to the Fulfillment of Your Dreams.* (Novato, CA: New World Library and San Rafael, CA: Amber-Allen Publishing, 1994).

53. Meyer, *Setting the Table.*

54. Bale and Doneen, *Beat the Heart Attack Gene.*

55. Richard Carlson, *Don't Sweat the Small Stuff . . . and It's All Small Stuff: Simple Ways to Keep the Little Things from Taking Over Your Life* (New York, NY: Hachette Books, 1997).

56. Andy Andrews. *The Little Things: Why You Really Should Sweat the Small Stuff* (Nashville, TN: Thomas Nelson, 2017).

57. Walter Willett. *Eat, Drink, and Be Healthy: The Harvard Medical School Guide to Healthy Eating* (New York, NY: Free Press, 2001).

58. Bruce Roseman and Kenneth Paul Rosenberg, *The Addictocarb Diet: Avoid the 9 Highly Addictive Carbs While Eating Anything Else You Want* (Dallas, TX: BenBella Books, 2015).

About the Author

Dr. Michael Sonick is an internationally known, highly regarded authority in dental implantology and periodontology. Having completed his undergraduate degree at Colgate University, he received his DMD at the University of Connecticut School of Medicine and his certificate in periodontology at Emory University. He received his implant training at Harvard University as well as the Brånemark Clinic in Gothenburg, Sweden.

A full-time practicing periodontist in Fairfield, Connecticut, Sonick is also a frequent guest lecturer in the international program at New York University School of Dentistry and the University of Connecticut School of Dental Medicine. He lectures worldwide on aesthetic implants, periodontal plastic surgery, guided bone regeneration, and comprehensive treatment planning. He is the coeditor of the multi-language textbook *Implant Site Development*, also translated into Spanish and Chinese. He serves on the editorial boards of numerous journals, including the *Compendium of Continuing Education, Inside Dentistry, Dentistry Today,* and the *Journal of Cosmetic Dentistry,* and he has published papers in peer-reviewed journals.

He is the founder and director of the Fairfield County Dental Club. This advanced continuing education organization provides courses on the latest developments in dentistry to clinicians and their staff. Dr. Sonick is also the founder and director of Sonick Seminars, LLC, a multidisciplinary teaching institute located in his clinical office and teaching center.

His international contributions have been recognized through various awards, including an honorary membership in the Indian Society of Periodontists, fellowship in the American College of Dentists, fellowship in the Pierre Fauchard Society, DentalXP mentor, and a member of *Who's Who in Dentistry*. The general dental practice residents at Yale New Haven Hospital also awarded Dr. Michael Sonick the honor of "Teacher of the Year." He has also been recognized as a Leader in Continuing Education by *Dentistry Today* for several years.

Dr. Sonick is a diplomate of the American Board of Periodontology, a diplomate of the International Congress of Oral Implantology, a fellow of the International Team for Implantology, a fellow of the International Society of Periodontal Plastic Surgeons, a member of the Leading Dental Centers of the World, and an Eagle Scout.

Dr. Sonick lives in Fairfield, Connecticut, and in Manhattan with his wife, Carole.

Discover Tips, Tools, and Tactics

Connect with Michael Sonick, DMD

PeopleNotPatients.org

Our Practice Is More than a Series of Procedures

Experience the Human Approach to Dental Health

At Fairfield County Implants and Periodontics,

our patients are treated with the

utmost care and compassion.

Discover More:

PeopleNotPatients.org

Treating People Not Patients Online Course

Discover the Proven Process to Develop a State-of-the-Art Practice

High-Quality Care Experiences for People and Practitioners

PeopleNotPatients.org/course

Go Deeper with *Treating People Not Patients*

Invite Dr. Michael Sonick to Speak to Your Organization

"Dr. Sonick has captured the bellwether of success in administering clinical practice. Through his vast experience, his learnings are shared through anecdotes, personal reflection, and strategic communication skills necessary to engage the binding trust that creates subjective value for our patients."

—Robert A. Faiella, DMD, MMSc, MBA
Past President, American Dental Association

PeopleNotPatients.org

BLOCKCHAIN
VERIFIED IP™

Powered by Easy IP™